The Fed,
the Markets,
and the
Metamorphosis
of the Business Cycle

A Christian Perspective

D1739223

The Fed,
the Markets,
and the
Metamorphosis
of the Business Cycle

A Christian Perspective

John E. Charalambakis, Ph.D.

FRANCIS ASBURY PRESS
of Evangel Publishing House

Nappanee, Indiana 46550

Toll-Free Order Line: (800) 253-9315
Internet Website: www.evangelpublishing.com

Biblical quotations, unless otherwise noted, are from the HOLY BIBLE, NEW INTERNATIONAL VERSION. Copyright © 1973, 1978, 1984 International Bible Society. Used by permission of Zondervan Publishing House.

This publication is designed to express the opinions of the author with regard to the subject matter covered. If legal advice, investment advice, or other expert assistance is required, the services of a competent professional person should be sought.

Cover design by Grand Design

Publisher's Cataloging-in-Publication Data
Charalambakis, John E.
  The Fed, the markets and the metamorphosis of the business cycle : a Christian perspective / John E. Charalambakis.
    p. cm.
    LCCN 2002102176
    ISBN 1-928915-31-0

  1. United States--Economic conditions--1981-2001. 2. United States--Economic conditions--2001- 3. United States--Economic policy--1993-2001. 4. United States--Economic policy--2001- 5. Business cycles. 6. Economics--Religious aspects--Christianity. I. Title.

HC106.82.C43 2002   330.973'0931
                    QBI02-200215

Printed in the United States of America
10 9 8 7 6 5 4 3 2 1

Table of Contents

Foreword

We live in a new economic era that is characterized by an explosion of information technology, new institutions, globalization, and uncertainty. In this new era, it is a challenge for us to move from fear to courage and take the challenge and the opportunity to transform our institutions (governmental, social, political, and economic) as well as our personal lives. This book is a call to personal and corporate transformation that is guided by our commitment to God and to the ideals that this country is founded on. It is a call to change because, unless we change, we are not faithful to the call to advance Christian standards, serving God and our fellow citizens.

This book integrates elements of current economic thought with biblical principles to give a balanced perspective with sound economic and spiritual foundations. Dr. Charalambakis' predictions about the markets have been correct and sound. The economic trends the followed the presentation of each talk have validated Dr. Charalambakis' insights. This book thus has significance for our evaluation of future economic conditions.

In these days it is immensely important for us to be informed about the governmental and economic conditions of our country and our world. Dr. Charalambakis provides good information integrated with spiritual sensitivity and shines a light on the happenings of the past in a way that will help us prepare for the future. I strongly recommend the reading of this book. It will deepen your understanding of the many elements of the changing world around us.

U.S. Representative Ernie Fletcher
Kentucky 6th District

Acknowledgments

Whatever the weaknesses of this book, they would have been far greater without the help of those who attended the presentations, asking questions, challenging my thoughts, and forcing me to think through the issues. I would like to extend a special thank you to Reverend Ron Smith, president of Wesley Biblical Seminary, for organizing many of the presentations. In addition, this book benefited significantly from the timely work of my editors, Joseph D. Allison and Mary Friedeman. I am grateful to them for their suggestions and efficiency.

My colleagues at Asbury College and my students were also very encouraging and helpful with their comments and suggestions.

My family stood behind me while these essays were written and through my extensive travel schedule. This book is dedicated to my wife, Fedra, God's greatest earthly gift. I really do not know of any other person who exemplifies sacrificial love more than my beloved spouse.

Introduction

The reality of the business cycle and the economic experience of individuals, corporations, and nations is an experience of metamorphosis. Actually, our entire lives reflect the reality of metamorphosis. Societies and economies that refuse to change decline and are disgraced. We are made for metamorphosis. Empires have come and gone. Corporations rise and go bankrupt. The thesis of these essays is that we must change; we cannot remain the same.

Every morning we wake up even though, during the night, some of our body cells died and new ones were born. The moment that this cycle ceases, we die. This death and regeneration experience produces life. Life itself is made up of regenerative cycles. At any moment, some cycles come to completion and new cycles begin. The baby is born and soon starts crawling and walking and playing with the neighborhood kids. Then school starts, then college, and suddenly you realize that the infant you were holding in your hands now holds a baby instead.

The cycles of life are starting points for new beginnings. We are in constant need of these new beginnings. They are causes of jubilation. We celebrate with excitement the prospects that are opening before us. However, when life's cycles are abruptly interrupted, crisis hits and the new beginning is overshadowed with sorrow and sadness. The ultimate outcome of the new cycle usually depends upon our responses to the crisis. Can we find good in the bad? Can we see the big picture? Can we discern that this crisis is just one bad chapter in a wonderful book?

Economists often use the term *business cycles* to represent the ups and downs of an economy. During the upswings of the business cycle (the boom times), prosperity spreads, incomes rise, spending increases, unemployment drops, production increases, deficits decline, profits increase, the equity (stock) markets rejoice, trade expands, and overcapacity is built (which sometimes becomes the seed for an economic bust). On the other hand, during the downturns of the business cycle, unemployment rises, production falls, incomes drop, spending declines, inventories accumulate, trade contracts, profits decline, and the equity markets experience losses.

As with every cycle in life, business cycles reach a point when they are "full of days" and their end is imminent. Individuals, organizations, and nations that refuse to prepare for this reflect the sort of mentality that says the earth is flat and we will never experience a sunset. Whether we prepare for the sunset or not, we will live in darkness sometime. The metamorphosis of the day into night (and vice versa) is an opportunity for constructive change.

For example, the beginning of the twentieth century found Argentina a vibrant economy full of life, free of debt, an exporter of goods, a magnet for capital (both physical and financial), and with a business cycle characterized by high levels of production, employment, income, and profit. At the beginning of the twenty-first century, Argentina struggles to restructure its debts, its competitiveness has declined, and its people experience high levels of unemployment. What went wrong?

In the late 1980s, economists, political scientists, and other intellectuals were predicting the rise of Japan as the new economic superpower. In that spirit, Paul Kennedy of Yale University published in 1987 the book *The Rise and Fall of the Great Powers*. However, although the Japanese economy and its market (which, as any market, is nothing but a discounted forecast of future earnings) hit its high in December 1989 when the Nikkei Index stood at 38,000. However, by the end of 2001 the Japanese economy had experienced four recessions and record-high unemployment rates. Japan had changed prime ministers six times, several of its celebrated banks were insolvent, and the Nikkei Index stood barely above the 11,000 level! What went wrong?

The decline of European nation-states before the Middle Ages, as well as of the Middle Eastern and Oriental empires, reflects the importance of vision for change. Those nations lacked visionary leadership to anticipate the upcoming changes, prepare for them, and build a solid foundation for a new economic cycle.

The recognition of an economic turning point is vital in order to comprehend the significance of cycles in our personal and corporate lives and to prepare for the consequences that those cycles have for us and our communities. The joys, sorrow, and hopes that come from each new economic cycle are signs of regeneration. If we refuse to change, we miss the turning point and the opportunity it holds.

Each new cycle starts with death. Unless we let the old die, we cannot enjoy the life of the newborn one. Jesus reminds us that unless a seed dies in the ground, we should not expect any kind of fruit (John 12:24). Life only comes from death, and we have received eternal life through Jesus' death and resurrection. This sacrificial love of Christ is a call for metamorphosis in our personal and corporate lives. We cannot live with the losses of the past.

The Bible proclaims that when we live in daily communion with God, our transformed lives can find redemption through the liberating risks of discipleship.

Individuals and organizations need to change by virtue of the losses they experience. We need to embrace regeneration and transcend what lies behind. Persons and corporations who understand that we cannot change our situation but we can allow our situation to change us are the ones who experience the new cycles of life that turn bad into good through the medium of God's grace. Grace does not change the moral order. What is bad will remain bad. However, grace takes our losses and turns them into a blessing. That is what God accomplished through Jesus' crucifixion. He turned the evil act of an unjust murder into the good of salvation, because nothing can separate us from God's love (Rom. 8:39).

Around 1997-1998, we were hearing in the United States the voices of various economists proclaiming that the business cycle was dead. The information technology revolution and the dot-coms had carried the equity markets to astonishing highs. We read of the Dow Jones Industrial Average at 3,600 in 1993 and in 1999 of the Dow at 10,000! Only in a Monopoly game could someone realize earnings more quickly. However, the exuberance of the Internet frenzy was reaching the end of its natural cycle and that bubble was about to burst.

By late 1999, we saw the first signs of trouble. These signs included (but were not limited to) unused plant capacity, declining corporate profits, high corporate debt levels, overspent consumers, and a glut in industrial production. At the same time, the Federal Reserve ("the Fed") was refusing to recognize those signs. The Fed was blind to the fact that an economic turning point had been reached and a new cycle had already started. Fed Chairman Alan Greenspan spoke of trying to achieve a "soft landing." (That comment made me think we were in a mythic kind of odyssey, having set sail without knowing where we were and without understanding what was happening at the home front.) Thus, my first essay, "The Odyssey of Creative Destruction," called for a cleansing fire to rid the economy of the elements that sapped its energy, like the suitors who wasted Odysseus's home resources.

In late 2000, the majority of the economy's analysts were calling for a V-shaped recovery. A few were saying it might take longer; thus, they predicted a U-shaped recovery. Looking at the excess capacity in the U.S. economy, along with the declining profits, unstable productivity gains, declining consumer confidence, frozen capital spending, and the instability of the global financial picture, I decided in late 2000 to write the essay titled "Economic Outlook for 2001." It explained that we were not destined for either a "soft" or "hard" landing. We were beginning a bumpy ride that could result in an L-shaped landing (a sudden drop, followed by economic stagnation).

Unfortunately, that prediction was verified week after week. The markets kept going down, corporations kept cutting their capital expenditures, investments declined fast, and the Fed danced alone by cutting interest rates without comprehending that the root of the problem was not monetary. Thus, in February 2001, I wrote another essay, on "Strategic Thinking and the Message of the Markets," suggesting that the monetary policy followed by the Fed and the corporate strategies seen in the equity markets reflected spasmodic reactions rather than thoughtful actions. I proposed that we should take into consideration the reality that overinvestment had led us into a recession, so the slowdown had been initiated by businesses' spending decline rather than by consumers' spending decline. This was the beginning of a nasty economic cycle, which had not been seen for at least seventy years. The essay warned that we must guard against the possibility of deflation, which unfortunately did occur later in the year.

By the spring of 2001, it seemed that we were dealing with a kind of economic virus that could take on catastrophic proportions. In my public presentation of the paper "On Viruses, Markets, Risks, and Visions" (as well as in my classroom lectures at Asbury College), I suggested that a serious global downturn was possible for the first time since World War II. In that essay, I explained that the global financial system suffers from a schizophrenic mentality of micromanagement that does not allow us to see the bigger picture but rather consumes its resources in wasteful narrow efforts that backfire and undermine the prospects for growth.

In early summer of 2001, I thought that the situation was maddening. I recalled the grim experience of Sir Isaac Newton in the opening of my essay titled "The Charms of the Market, the Sunset of 'The Madness of the People,' and the Dollar." The thesis of this piece was that, despite the clear signs of a new bust cycle that became nastier day by day, the Fed continued dancing alone. The essay presented an historical review to show that the Fed was trying to sustain an economic bubble and using monetary tools to fight a nonmonetary downturn and an inevitable new economic cycle. Therefore, the Fed's policy was undermining the value of the dollar.

By late summer 2001, higher unemployment and declining consumer confidence started hitting home. The essay "Mortgaging Our Economic Future" dealt with the bubble in the housing sector and claimed that this bubble was the one that sustained consumer spending. Once this bubble burst, however, the economy would go into a tailspin, whose end could not be predicted at that point. The essay advised readers to practice careful asset allocation and suggested that the bumpy ride would last longer than anticipated.

All of a sudden, our world changed on September 11, 2001. An inviting inner voice called for something new, for a new experience as a people. Our souls cried at the losses, but our spirits were not crushed. Our hopes did not die and our dreams did not vanish. That morning of terrorism marked the birth of Americans' new beginning as a people. The metamorphosis that was needed finally started to appear. Nations die when they fail to change. Communities and organizations die when they fail to respond with a renewed spirit and vision to the challenges and tragedies of their times. Unless we allow our losses to transform us, we exacerbate our suffering and slowly but definitely drift into the second death, the destruction of our spirits. The first death happens to us, but the second death happens in us. When individuals, corporations, and nations bemoan their losses and fail to embrace the necessary changes that the losses require, they lose their vision. Without vision, people simply die (Prov. 29:18).

In the midst of the pessimism that prevailed in economic circles immediately after the terrorist attacks, I wrote and presented the essay "From Fear to Courage" in October 2001. I outlined the turning points in our economy and explained why, based on those twelve signs, the recession would not last long if the economy was properly managed. I further predicted that global recession probably would be avoided and that a transformational cycle had started that would reverse the trends up to that point.

Finally, in early November 2001, I wrote and presented the essay "The Three Cs of the New Cycle." In my presentation, I actually spoke of six Cs-Chasms, Cycles, Cocoons, Catharsis, Catalysts, and Circumcision. The essay explains why we are indeed in a new economic upswing and encourages individuals to take a contrarian view of the economy. Chasms usually reflect the start of a new cycle, in which periods of apparent economic dormancy are actually cocoons where significant change may be occuring. The new cycle requires catharsis and a catalyst for the necessary changes to take place. However, without the experience which God calls the circumcision of the heart (Rom. 2:28-29)—that moment in our personal and corporate lives when we are not only regenerated but marked for God's use alone—a person lives without clear goals and objectives, which may lead to a loss of vision for the future.

The book concludes with an article that I wrote more than two years ago as the fruit of extensive research. I called it the "Political Economy of the Kingdom of God," and it reflects my thoughts about how we as individuals, as well as members of institutions and organizations, need to incorporate the reality of God's kingdom in our actions, ideals, goals, and economic policies. It will probably be perceived as the most controversial chapter of this book. I surely hope so!

John E. Charalambakis
Asbury College
Wilmore, Kentucky

The Odyssey of Creative Destruction

Presented October 2000

In chapter 19 of the *Odyssey*, Homer writes about Penelope's encounter with a mysterious guest: "Falsehoods all, but he gave his falsehoods all the ring of truth. As she listened on, her tears flowed and soaked her cheeks as the heavy snow melts down from the high mountain ridges." Later, in chapter 22, when the guest proves to be Penelope's long-missing husband, Odysseus, and his fighting of Penelope's suitors is almost done, Odysseus proclaims, "Fire first.…Light me a fire to purify this house.'…Odysseus purges his palace, halls and court, with cleansing fumes."

A few years ago, the gurus of the financial marketplace proclaimed that a new era had arrived. They said it was the dawn of the New Economy. That new era was said to defy the old laws of economics. The New Economy supposedly had no limits to its growth potential. We heard that is was an economy where inflation was dead, an economy where smooth landings were assured and where the Dow could climb to 36,000. Why not to 100,000?

In this New Economy, we were told, the Odysseus of the American character had left Troy and was finally coming home. The question, of course, was how long it would take him to come home and what kind of a home would he find. His wife, Penelope, allowed her suitors to dream big dreams of palaces, fame, and wealth—while Odysseus was conversing with Athena.

In chapter 13 of the *Odyssey* we read their dialogue: "Royal son of Laertes, Odysseus, old campaigner, think how to lay your hands on all those brazen suitors, lording it over your house now, three whole years, courting your noble wife, offering gifts to win her. But she, forever, brokenhearted for your return, builds up each man's hopes—dangling promises, dropping hints to each—but all the while with something else in mind." And as the dialogue continues, Odysseus asks Athena to help him deal with the men who were wasting his resources. Athena urges him, "First I will transform you—no one must know you." Odysseus needed a metamorphosis.

Yes, the American Odysseus has been transformed, but he remains Odysseus, looking for his family, his friends and associates, his palace, and his belongings. He always remains the man of intrigue. I feel sorry for those who cannot understand Odysseus is back with us. The old economy is not dead. The New Economy is the old one in new clothes; it has been transformed but it is still the same, ready to teach its lessons to those who will listen. Yes, we have been experiencing higher economic growth; yes, Penelope has been whispering in our ears, dangling promises and building up our hopes; but please remember, she still has something else in mind.

Where is the economy's vaunted transformation coming from? Look at its new technologies; new waves of globalization; new financial instruments; new democracies; new global organizations dedicated to promoting trade, peace, stability, and prosperity; new venture capital firms ready to fund the e-economy; and an ever-new Alan Greenspan. Isn't that marvelous?

Let's try to follow the rationale of the New Economy: Technological innovations accelerate the rate of productivity growth, which, in combination with globalization, forces everyone to cut costs and promote efficiency and competition (both of which keep inflation down and boost economic growth), which in turn translates into higher incomes, higher employment levels and higher spending. Therefore, proponents of the New Economy say we have entered a phase of unlimited growth. Traditional valuation methods are obsolete. Expect big gains. Do not worry about the bottom line. The e-economy will generate abundant profits in the future. Our strategy now is just to buy losers at unprecedented bargain prices. No doubt we have new engines of growth. The only question is, do we have the fuel to run those engines?

I believe that we are overimpressed by current innovations and mesmerized by the gurus proclaiming new eras. We are all speculators now; at least that's the whisper in our ears. We act on emotions rather than rationality. Needless to say, we often do not understand how things work. We use financial leverage for short-term gains without understanding its long-term implications. The overextension of credit builds a conspiracy of trust that becomes obsolete within a few months. Then who will pay back the capital?

Our exuberance leads us to overinvest in areas that cannot produce a sustained return (e.g., the telecommunications industry). Is there enough demand to absorb such floods of investment? Is the income sufficient to support such profit margins? Supply does not create its own demand. Oversupply simply begins to destroy the current system. Yes, that may be a form of creative destruction, which may be necessary. However, when we lose control of the supply, the outcome is not always desirable.

The ship of the American economy has left the harbor but does not have a destination. Worse yet, just as it left the port its compass went bad, but the first mate refuses to return to the harbor. And when the first mate (i.e., the chairman of the Fed), who has led the ship through so much turbulence before, is asked, "Have you no care for him in your lofty heart? Did he never win your favor with sacrifices?" the Olympian responds, "My child,…what nonsense you let slip through your teeth. Now, how on earth could I forget Odysseus?"

Moreover, the problem compounds when we grasp the fact that the first mate has lost not only the destination and the compass but also the realization that he no longer has control of the ship. You see, it is one thing to lose your way—you may eventually arrive at your intended destination by accident. It is another thing for something to go wrong—equipment does fail. But it is dangerous not to recognize those facts and still insist that you have control of the ship.

Fresh money supply cannot be dropped into this new global village from a helicopter, and the sooner we recognize that, the better off we will be. Money has become a variable controlled by the financial system, which has the ability to generate new financial instruments on a global scale. The new system-generated money expands credit (in some instances unconditionally, based on exuberant expectations), which in turn is overinvested, creating higher expectations of return.

We need to fully comprehend the role that venture capital plays in the New Economy. Ten years ago, venture capital barely funded $5 billion worth of new projects. Now this amount surpasses $100 billion a year. In addition, initial public offerings (IPOs) of corporate stock have become a source of system-generated financing that surpasses what anyone could have imagined just five years ago. The combination of plentiful venture capital and questionable IPOs creates new monies outside of the traditional financial framework. So the money supply has become an uncontrolled endogenous variable.

This overinvestment forces the old system to die—even if it is not yet its time to die—and thus we prematurely create something new. The pace of innovation surpasses the sustainable growth rate of the economy and does not allow the markets to digest the new technologies. We have not allowed the normal technological lags to work, and thus the capital market is congested with innovations that it does not know what to do with. As the market slows down to breathe, sales cannot meet the investors' higher expectations. Disappointments prevail, stock prices drop, funding becomes less available, innovation decreases, conflicts arise, productivity slows, costs and breakeven points increase, prices rise, and thus higher inflation rates make their appearance.

We can easily understand why, from that point onward, capital is destroyed and recession is at hand. Inflation does not occur when too much money chases too few goods, but rather when conflicting interests make claims over a limited pie that cannot increase in size. When the pie expands, conflicting interests are satisfied as long as their shares remain about the same. Therefore, when capital spending expands, variables such as productivity, growth, employment, and incomes experience increases, conflicts are reduced, and inflation is kept in check. However, when things turn around, heterogeneous groups assert their conflicting claims, businesses go bankrupt, mergers take place, employees lose their jobs, the government raises taxes, the level of competition reduced, efficiencies are decreased, and costs naturally rise.

It is abnormal to experience inflation in the New Economy because inflation is the mirror image of self-interest. During the good times, self-interest becomes homogeneous. However, when the climate of over-investment and overcapitalization turns sour because of unmet expectations, self-interest becomes a heterogeneous variable that is the seed for the destruction of that business cycle. The arena of conflict raises power in disproportional ways among the economic agents. As long as the dynamics of the economy (e.g., competition, exuberance, investment, and consumption) keep the conflict at a stable level, homogeneity of self-interests will prevail. However, when the dynamics change, conflicting interests redistribute power unequally and the trouble starts.

You see, as long as Odysseus was perceived to be gone, his wife's suitors had a common self-interest. But when Odysseus returned, their self-interests became as diverse as their number. Of course, their homogeneous self-interest had destroyed the estate, but that is another story. (In chapter 17 of the *Odyssey*, we read: "But they, they infest our palace day and night, they butcher our cattle, our sheep, our fat goats, feasting themselves sick, swilling our glowing wine as if there is not tomorrow—all of it, squandered. No, there is no man like Odysseus in command to drive this curse from this house…if only Odysseus came back home")

King Menelaus offered Telemachus some fine horses for the return trip to Ithaca, but the young man politely refused, saying his homeland could not support them. Like Telemachus, we are given horses to take back to Ithaca, but our Ithaca is not ready for horses, at least not yet. The excitement of those stallions and all the transactions to put them on the ship generate growth. You see, the boom generated by new investment monies is planting seeds, and those seeds are being watered by the overexcited investors to create a boom in the economy. The stallions are wonderful, so let's take them on. They say the problem is that not even the ship can handle them. We cannot sustain that weight; we simply cannot have continuous abnormal returns. Sooner or later, the financial returns will revert to their normal (if not to below-normal) levels and the boom will become a bust. If we overcapitalize our economy, we will lose control of the cost. That in turn will reduce the level of operating efficiencies (both on macro and micro levels) which, when combined with the excessive leverage due to new monies and financial instruments, will cause stakeholders' dissatisfaction an non-performing (bad) loans. It will be time to turn off the lines of credit—but that may be too little and too late.

We cannot expect a garden to yield fruit on a constant basis. There is no such thing as Phaeacia's gardens (chapter 7 in the *Odyssey*), where "the yield of all these trees will never flag or die, neither in winter nor in summer, a harvest all year round" But observe how Odysseus reacted to the unprecedented garden in front of him: "He crossed the threshold quickly, strode inside the palace. Here he found the Phaeacian lords" He asked not for a share of their bounty but, "as for myself, grant me a rapid convoy home to my own native land. How far away I have been from my loved ones…how long I have suffered!"

You see, Odysseus knew his destination. Odysseus explained to his listeners how he had met Calypso, who "took me in in all her kindness, welcomed me warmly, cherished me, even vowed to make me immortal, ageless, all my days—but she never won the heart inside me, never. Seven endless years I remained there, always drenching with my tears the immortal clothes Calypso gave me. Then at last…she saw me on my way in a solid craft tight and trim, and gave me full provisions…" Unlike this noble traveler, we have allowed ourselves to be seduced by the premise of more and more. The problem takes on greater proportions because we have placed all our confidence in the first mate of the ship, who has lost his way. Japan has been experiencing a similar problem.

Since late 1989, Japan has lowered its key interest rate to practically zero and its economy does not move. It is foolish to expect that by lowering interest rates we will be able to overcome all of our economic problems. The Japanese have been trying that for a decade. I fear that the world is in for several years of uncertainty, instability, and downturn under the mismanagement of our beloved first mate, who refuses to see that a new cycle has started and who insists on applying the same old monetary solutions.

It is needless, of course, to mention the international implications of an economic downturn. International financial managers will rush to the exits. Then, as in chapter 21 of the *Odyssey*, "Odysseus…with his virtuoso ease strung his mighty bow. Quickly his right hand plucked the string to test its pitch and under his touch it sang out clear and sharp as a swallow's cry. Horror swept through the suitors, faces blanching white."

This massive exit—due to the huge current-account deficit that the United States now carries—will push the stock prices even lower. It will depress the value of the dollar, which will then be recognized as overvalued. What will our first mate do at that time? Raise interest rates to keep the dollar strong, in hopes of preventing this massive exit? Imagine no one buying America's goods and services, and our first mate's proclaiming that we can solve the problem by raising interest rates. And what about the European markets, not to mention Latin America, Asia, and the rest?

Economic phenomena do not indeed have only monetary roots. Economic phenomena also have moral roots; we need to understand that economics simply extends moral philosophy into the sphere of arranging all of life's priorities.

Individuals, organizations, and nations need a moment of truth in their personal and collective lives, a moment when they find themselves. We need a place of Peniel where we struggle with God as Jacob did in Genesis 32. We need to find who we really are and what we want from our lives. Human history was changed because Jacob found himself. In the midst of Jacob's running and looking over his shoulder for fear of his brother, Esau, God confronted him and asked him for his name (Gen. 32:27). Isn't it interesting that the

God of the universe would ask somebody for his name? What had happened the last time that somebody asked Jacob for his name? In Genesis 27:32, we find his earthly father Isaac asking Jacob for his name. Jacob replied, "Esau." In that moment, he lost himself. Decades later, when his heavenly Father asked the same question, Jacob was forced to find himself again. By doing so, the course of history was changed. The world was never the same from that point on!

Critical and pivotal changes in our lives start when we discover ourselves, like the Prodigal Son in Luke 15. The old self indeed needs to die, but this change cannot start until our minds change—what the Greeks call *metanoia*—which will lead to the abandonment of our old ways. Only then can renewal flourish and expand.

Does our economy really sail in a solid craft, tight and trim? Does it even have an anchor? Or have we lost our way?

Who will set the cleansing fire? Where is Peniel in our collective lives?

Projecting the Economic Outlook

Presented December 2000

Most of the analysts these days talk about a "soft landing" or a "hard landing" for the economy. I think that it would be safe to say that we are not in for any landing yet, whether hard or soft. I believe that the economic outlook for 2001 calls for a bumpy ride. We may then, by the end of the third quarter of 2001, be approaching a landing. Let me justify this conclusion by citing the follow characteristics:

1.) The net savings rate for the United States is low.

2.) The current-account deficit is growing.

3.) The debt ratio (for both corporations and individuals) in the United States is high.

4.) The stock market, by many standards, is still overvalued.

5.) The exchange rate for the dollar in relation to other major currencies signifies that it is overvalued.

6.) The interconnections between different economies in this "global village" will trigger economic trouble for other nations if growth in the United States slows down.

7.) The productivity growth gains that we have been experiencing in the last three or four years have slowed significantly, which will affect the outlook for 2001, especially if those productivity gains prove to be cyclical rather than structural.

All the above signs reflect the reality of economic instability, which feeds uncertainty and risk. We need to remember that there is an economic Promised Land out there, although the journey to the Promised Land may be full of misadventures, instability, and disappointments. I believe we should look closer and try to identify the primary causes of the delays, the disappointments, and the uncertainties.

The old cartoon by Walt Kelly said that we have found the enemy and it is us! Our society has lost it focus. It seems that our nation's economic focus is nothing but the rationalization of our personal selfishness. We have made ourselves and our possessions the center of reality. By doing so, we have forgotten where the Promised Land is and what it is about. We have failed to experience the tranformative power of God for conversion of the heart, mind, and wallet!

In Mark 12, Jesus makes some significant comments about our intimate relationship with money. In Matthew 6:24, he clearly teaches that money is not an impersonal medium of exchange. The Nobel laureate Milton Friedman taught that money is neutral, in the sense that it cannot affect employment and output, but can only affect prices. Yet two thousand years before Friedman, Christ proclaimed that the neutrality of money is a myth. It deeply affects our lives. Unfortunately, money has become a deity. For many people, it is omnipresent and omnipotent. Many find security and power in their financial resources. Money is thought to reign supreme in all areas of life, even in the church! We need a new vision of the proper place and role of money in our lives. The volatility of our financial markets reflects the fact that our lives have lost spiritual focus and vision.

The Bumpy Ride Scenario

On December 5, 1996, Federal Reserve Chairman Alan Greenspan announced that the stock market was suffering from irrational exuberance. The market went south the next day. On the fourth anniversary of that famous talk, Mr. Greenspan delivered another speech to the Community Bankers Association in New York, giving an upbeat scenario for the economy that uplifted the NASDAQ by a record 10.48 percent in one day and had analysts applauding that indeed we are in for a soft landing, that market volatility and decline were over and the United States economy was stronger than ever.

We should observe that the volatility in the financial markets has increased uncertainty in both the economic sphere (regarding the growth rate of the economy) and in the financial sphere (regarding expectations about the equity markets, profitability, spending, and the strength of the dollar.)

This volatility mirrors the underlying worries of the American economy as well as the global economy. These underlying worries are based on the following statistical indicators:

1.) We see a significant volatility in the growth rate of our productivity.

2.) We see increases in unemployment insurance claims.

3.) Orders for durable goods have fallen significantly in the last few months.

4.) Inventories have been accumulating in the past two quarters, and inventory accumulation reflects that we face declining demand in the market.

5.) We see profitability being squeezed by a combination of lower demand and higher production costs.

6.) Capital spending has declined by more than 20 percent in the last five months.

Mr. Greenspan and the Fed clearly are targeting a soft landing for the economy. However, the historical evidence is against such a soft landing for the reasons that we considered previously.

A New Kind of Financial Instability

By raising interest rates by almost two hundred basis points in the last eighteen months, Mr. Greenspan is trying to slow down demand in both the capital and the consumer markets. However, this excessive guiding of the markets may have the effect of slowing down the economy. Therefore, it would not be a surprise if we were to see the growth rate of the economy falling to between 1.5 and 2 percent in the next three quarters. Given the fact that the economy was growing at a rate of over 4 percent in recent years, this kind of slowdown will feel like a recession. If this indeed takes place, the slowdown will deflate expectations in the market. Those deflated expectations will have a negative effect, which may lead to an even bigger slowdown in the economy and bigger cuts in spending— capital spending as well as consumer spending—which may lead the economy in the third quarter of 2001 into a real recession, when GDP actually starts declining rather than rising.

The above indicators and the phenomena that I explained earlier point to the fact that we have economic and financial imbalances in the country, that leave the economy vulnerable to recession and financial instability. The deflation that we have been observing in capital markets has erased more than $2 trillion of American wealth; therefore, the excessive optimism that has prevailed in the markets may soon be replaced by excessive pessimism.

This turnover of expectations in the markets will be reflected in the credit markets, where credit will dry up. As investors start fleeing those markets (i.e., getting out of risk), it will be much more expensive for corporations to raise funds. A decline in lending will have an adverse effect on both corporate profitability and expectations, as well as on employment. We can clearly see that the credit market is in for trouble by looking at the spread between the interest rate on government securities and the yield of a junk bond. In recent months, this spread has been increasing, even by historical standards. The high rates paid on low-grade corporate bonds reflect the inability of new firms to attract investors, and to finance expansion and capital spending.

At the same time, we observe that the IPO market has been largely closed. Thousands of banks in the United States, as shown in a recent survey of the Federal Reserve, have been raising their lending standards to unnecessary levels. Actually, those conservative lending standards and the growing number of nonproductive loans are the highest since late 1990, when we were in our last recession.

It is interesting also to note that this tightening reflects a deterioration in the credit quality of the applicants. Lending to commercial firms has been growing by less than 2 percent annually in the last two quarters, compared with an annual growth of at least 12 percent a year and a half ago. The excessive debt-to-equity ratio of many corporations threatens the commercial banks if the loans they make turn out to be non-productive.

The Fed is extremely nervous, because the prosperity of the last six years has been bought on credit, through easy access to financial markets and speculative capital spending.

Of course, capital spending and easy access to capital are not the only two forces of economic growth. Other forces include consumer spending (which makes up about two-thirds of our GDP), globalization, and information technology. Let's examine those three forces, beginning with globalization.

Several human-rights organizations have turned against globalization and its potential threats to economic and social well-being. This backlash has been increasing in size and influence since late 1999. Yet we can be sure that national economies will become more globally interdependent as we move forward.

Information technology spending is another variable that merits attention. Businesses and governments have sharply reduced their purchases of new technology.

Capital spending of all kinds has been declining significantly in the last year. So if we take a hard look at all of the forces that have been driving the economy since 1994, we can see that all of them are in a declining mode. This naturally leads to the "bumpy ride" scenario.

Financial Instability and Productivity Growth

The prevailing uncertainty in the markets will continue for at least the next five to six months. Let me reiterate the significance of business investment: this has almost doubled as a share of GDP in the last decade. At the beginning of 1992, business investment as a share of GDP was barely 9 percent. At the beginning of the year 2000, it was almost 17 percent. The growth rate of capital investments in the last four years has been 26 percent; however, that growth rate has slowed down in the last ten months to a little over 7 percent. This significant drop in capital investment has serious consequences for productivity, and this is a major issue that we need to address. I believe that the drop in capital spending will have negative consequences for our productivity, which may affect inflation, interest rates, the strength of the economy, and, of course, the strength of the currency. Let me take those things one by one.

In the 1970s and 1980s, the United States experienced dismal productivity growth rates. To a large extent, the economic landscape was affected by its poor performance. When our productivity growth rate is not sufficient, supplies can no longer meet demand, and inflation comes into the picture. The resulting decline in purchasing power of both suppliers and consumers has a corrosive effect on the economic environment.

In the 1990s, we saw the opposite scenario. We had a significant increase in productivity growth that exceeded 3 percent in the mid-1990s and has registered over 4 percent since mid-1997. A strong investment climate has lifted productivity and helped to keep inflation down. When the equity markets see more investment, higher productivity, and lower inflation, they applaud because they expect that profits will be boosted and therefore stock prices will increase. The effect of all these factors is that the cost of raising capital is substantially lower. Therefore, long-term interest rates in the bond markets (where they are determined) are declining.

Furthermore, when the cost of capital is declining, investments increase. In turn, this leads to higher productivity gains. Some may say that this "new" reality that we saw in the 1990s has created a new economic multiplier. To test whether that is true, let me go over the various factors of this "new multiplier" again.

Information-technology spending and capital-investment spending have lifted up productivity, which has kept inflation down, pushed corporate profits and stock prices higher, and reduced the cost of capital by reducing long-term interest rates. This has encouraged further capital spending, which in turn has pushed productivity growth rates higher. In that sense, productivity increases are both structural (due to technological advancements) and cyclical (moving along with the upswing of the business cycle).

However, the critical question is this: Which part of productivity growth is stronger, the structural or the cyclical? If it is the latter, then the effects of an economic downturn will be felt on a larger scale and most of the gains made in the last few years will be jeopardized.

Productivity Growth, the "New Multiplier," and the Strength of the Dollar

Where does the strength of the currency fit in? We must always remind ourselves that the strength of the currency is nothing but a measure of the strength of the economy. The reality of the higher growth rate in the United States has created an environment of confidence. Therefore, the dollar has become increasingly strong in the last three to four years.

A stronger dollar, of course, holds down inflation because imports become less expensive. At the same time, a stronger dollar attracts foreign capital to the United States, due to the fact that more foreigners wish to invest in U.S. securities (both bonds and stocks), since they have high confidence in the prospects of the U.S. economy.

The "bumpy ride" scenario becomes more credible when we take into account the following sequence of events: Falling stock markets will reduce expectations, downgrade confidence in the U.S. economy, raise the cost of capital, dry up the credit markets, and therefore reduce investment spending. This in turn will slow down the productivity growth rate, which will slow down corporate profit growth rate and depress share prices even more.

At the same time, slower productivity growth raises unit labor costs. Therefore, we may see in the near future higher inflation rates, which will make it extremely hard for the Fed to lower interest rates. The tight labor market that we have seen in the last three years has been counterbalanced by higher productivity. However, if this productivity growth rate slows down, wage costs will go up. This would lead to slower growth in the economy, pushing the dollar down and further undermining the Fed's ability to cut interest rates.

I mentioned earlier that the key to this forecast is the productivity growth rate. Let me explain one more reason why this is so important. As mentioned earlier, the productivity growth rate may be split into two components. One is cyclical and the other is structural. My fear is that the growth rate in productivity that we have been seeing lately is more cyclical than structural. This means that productivity growth rates move with the economic cycle; therefore, when there is business confidence in the economy, productivity growth accelerates. However, when the economy slows down, the productivity growth rate decreases. If indeed our recent productivity gains are related to cyclical factors and we then see the economy slowing down, we are most definitely going to see a productivity slowdown. This will have major negative consequences for the economic well-being of the United States.

On the other hand, if the productivity gains have been of a structural nature—i.e., indicating that the whole economy has changed its structure—then those productivity gains are here to stay. We will not be able to make a final call on this until the economy actually begins slowing down, but my assessment is that the productivity gains of the last twenty-four months have been primarily cyclical. Therefore, when the economic slowdown continues for the next four to six months, our productivity gains will be substantially reduced. Here it is important to remember the main thesis of our previous discussion, that creative destruction is created by overinvestment. Booms create busts, because the overinvestment creates excess capacity in the economy. When firms realize that their inventories have started accumulating, they slash their investment spending. As a result, the economy starts slowing down. At this stage, someone may raise a very logical question: "Why is the probability for a soft landing so low?" I believe that a soft landing at this stage of the economic cycle is not likely for two reasons:

1.) Historically speaking, a soft landing has rarely been accomplished. And in those times that the Fed may claim to have accomplished it, the results have been dismal.

2.) Slowing economies are much more vulnerable to shocks than strong economies. A shock such as higher wage cost, higher production cost (because of oil or material price increases), or another foreign stock market crisis will make the soft-landing scenario very difficult. We need to remember that in the late 1980s when we were talking about another soft landing, oil prices spiked upward and the savings-and-loan debacle dried up the credit markets. This brought down several financial institutions.

Exuberant Excesses

In this section, I would like to briefly touch on a few excesses that I observe in the marketplace. First of all, a careful look at the valuations of particular stock shares reveals that, from a historical perspective, we still see high price/earnings (P/E) ratios that are not warranted by the macrodynamics of a given industry. However, another matter that deserves as much attention is the ratio between market capitalization and Gross Domestic Product (GDP). Market capitalization typically averages between 85 percent and 110 percent of the GDP. In other words with a current GDP of $10 trillion, the market capitalization needs to be between $8.5 trillion and 11 trillion. Market capitalization today is close to $20 trillion. Therefore, the ratio of market capitalization to GDP is 2.0 rather than the historical average of 0.85–1.1. This excess in the capital markets is a sign of disturbance and imbalance.

Under these circumstances, if we have a slowdown in the economy, the market is much more vulnerable than if we had a market capitalization close to historical standards. This financial imbalance is close related to the negative personal savings rate and the corporate debt-to-equity ratio, as well as to the nation's current-account deficit in the following manner. First, venture capitalists' overinvestment, along with the rising stock market, has encouraged households to save less of their current income. Therefore, the private sector is running a record financial deficit, which is the difference between the savings rate of households and firms and their investment rate. This financial deficit is approaching 6 percent of GDP, which is a record level. If the household savings rate corrects and comes back to historical norms, we will see a sharp fall in demand as consumer spending and investor spending are reduced. However, if the economy slows significantly now, households have no cushion of savings to fall back on. The consequences—in terms of reduced spending, confidence, and investment—will be dramatic.

Second, market capitalization in relation to the GDP is directly related to the debt that households and companies have been accumulating in the last five to seven years. Private sector debt is at the record level of 150 percent of the GDP. Many say that this number is overestimated because at the same time stock prices have gone up. However, stock gains are paper gains, while debit is fixed in value. If there is a need to call in this private sector debt to be paid immediately, the stock market will suffer substantial losses.

The third perspective on this excess exuberance is the unfortunate fact that America is borrowing approximately 35 percent of its debt from overseas, attracting foreign capital in order to finance its current-account deficit. As long as the economy is growing and investment returns are high, it is easy to attract foreign capital. However, when investment spending and profits slow down, these dollar-denominated assets will be less and less attractive to international investors.

Furthermore, when the economy slows down, the value of the dollar will necessarily decline. This will not only make the Fed's task of lowering interest rates even harder, but it will also be much more difficult to raise capital from abroad. Foreign investors will withdraw their funds from the United States. This will inhibit growth and slow down the economy even further, not to mention depressing the stock market more.

All of these imbalances (financial and economic) create the need for fine-tuning the economy. However, the question is: Do we have the political and economic leadership capable of adjusting all of these imbalances to produce a positive result for the good of the American people?

Conclusion

I started this presentation by mentioning the effect of Mr. Greenspan's talk to the Community Bankers Association on December 5, 1996. At the close, let me elaborate further by saying that Mr. Greenspan may even be part of the moral hazard that we have been observing in the United States. I say "moral hazard" because Mr. Greenspan's talk of supporting the equity markets and of engineering a soft landing, as well as his personal tendency to support the market with his visible hand, eventually encourages investors to take more risks than necessary. They believe that the Fed always will intervene and lower interest rates when the economy goes down or the stock market suffers substantial losses. Such illusory hope has increased the risk level in the economy and has contributed to the high levels of debt, as well as to the current-account deficit, the high market capitalization relative to the GDP, and the negative net savings in the U.S. economy. If indeed the U.S. economy slows down, what would that mean for the global economy? America's GDP growth accounts for approximately 30 percent of global growth. If we added to that number the effect of

American imports, the United States is responsible for about 50 percent of global output and global growth. There are several channels through which a downturn in the United States will harm other economies. Among these are trade, exchange rates, and capital flows.

The United States absorbs billions of dollars' worth of imports from different countries such as Mexico, Canada, Japan, southeast Asia, and Europe. When the U.S. economy slows down, our imports from those countries and regions will slow down. Therefore, their growth rates will also slow down. The interrelatedness of trade implies that a slowdown in the United States may bring down other economies, too.

A scenario of the bumpy ride (or even worse, a hard landing) will be associated with a significant drop in the value of the dollar against other major currencies, primarily the Euro and the yen. That will positively affect our exports in the short term, but negatively affect the economies of other countries. Needless to say, if the dollar declines we may see higher inflation rates, more turmoil in the financial markets, and even higher interest rates at home. Of course, if this becomes a reality, the risk premiums and the yields on bonds will increase substantially and the credit market will dry up even further, making it more difficult for firms to raise capital.

In these scenarios, the Japanese economy would be affected much more than the European economies, because Japan has no room to lower the interest rates. In addition, the financial turmoil in Japan's banking sector leaves them unable to escape economic stagnation. The European economies may be in better shape because their capital markets are not overvalued as much as the U.S. markets. In addition, their growth rates will be running at approximately 2.5–3 percent next year, which is much higher than the Japanese growth rate.

The unfortunate thing is that the economies of emerging countries stand to lose the most from a hard landing or a bumpy ride for the United States. Economies in Latin America and Asia, which are driven primarily by export growth, will be severely hurt.

A slump in the United States will dry up their credit channels and may even necessitate some bankruptcies in those countries.

In conclusion, let me say that the probability of not having any landing yet is much higher than the probability of having either a hard or a soft landing. I encourage you to read Matthew 17:1–13 and reflect on the scene of Moses setting foot in the Promised Land, which God said that he could only see from a distance (Deut. 32:52). Perhaps the journey to our economic Promised Land will be delayed a bit longer, but I am confident we can yet reach that goal.

Strategic Thinking and the Message of the Markets

Presented February 2001

In this chapter, I would like to concentrate on two topics that have generated considerable interest in recent months. The first has to do with different scenarios of economic recovery. These scenarios depend on key factors in the global economy. The second has to do with some recommendations regarding the financial markets, particularly how we analyze stocks' performance in the next several months.

A general feeling of economic disappointment is being voiced in public discussions nowadays. That disappointment stems from unmet expectations, chiefly wrong expectations or irrational ones. The scene reminds me of Luke 24, where we find two followers of Christ walking toward the city of Emmaus and feeling very disappointed. Their hope was that Christ would free Israel, but He had been crucified. They were hoping that Jesus would kick out the Romans, unseat Pilate, and take control of their governments. However, the reality was that Pilate was still in and Jesus was dead. They felt the pain of unfulfilled expectations—God had not done what they wanted. But the kingdom of God is not about our expectations. God did not adjust His agenda to meet the disciples' wrong expectations. They wanted Jesus to redeem Israel politically, but God knew better. He would rather allow His people to be temporarily oppressed than eternally lost. When forced to choose between battling Pilate and battling Satan, God chose the battle we could not win. He said no to a politically liberated Israel and yes to a eternally liberated humanity. Aren't we glad He did so?

We too have wrong and irrational expectations today, and we would prefer to avoid even temporary pain that actually is a warning that something is wrong internally. Avoiding the pain and concentrating on wrong expectations can cause individuals and societies to lose their direction.

So why are we disappointed with our economy's performance? And what can we reasonably expect in the coming months?

Recovery Scenarios

First of all, we need to understand the dynamics of a V-shaped recovery of the economy, as well as the potential of a U-shaped recovery. These have been much discussed and debated. In previous essays, I sketched the problems facing the United States because of over-investment, overextension of credit, and a long overdue correction in the markets and in the economy. We should note that not all recessions are bad, and a healthy recession could be a good dose of medicine for the body politic that strengthens it and takes away viruses. Some analysts foresee V-shaped recovery, in which the economy experiences a sharp drop and then sharp growth. This kind of scenario definitely excludes the possibility of a soft landing. The V-shaped recovery scenario goes like this: The economy drops and the market drops; but then, by the second half of the year, the economy will experience a significant increase in output and a significant upturn in the financial markets. Then, all will be well.

I believe that a more realistic scenario would be one of a bumpy ride that ends with a U-shaped recovery. Here the economy slides an uneven rate toward the bottom and stays at the bottom a lot longer than anticipated. Then it experiences slow and painful growth because it takes a long time to recover from this drop. The danger in this scenario is that the drop might become a long-term slump. The obvious question: Is there an industrial country that has experienced the economic situation that the United States is going through right now, and where the U-shaped scenario became a long-term economic slump? The answer to that question is yes. We need look no farther than Japan. The Japanese economy is still struggling to recover from the slump that commenced in the late 1980s.

The Fed and the Future: What Can and What Should It Do?

This is the real danger, that the U-shaped economic slowdown turns into a slump. What can keep us out of this slump? Several columnists have written that Federal Reserve Chairman Alan Greenspan and his ability to manipulate interest rates are the key to preventing a scenario in which the recession becomes a slump. However, I believe that the days of Mr. Greenspan's ability to manipulate the markets are over or almost over. The reason lies in the expectations and anticipations of the people regarding the future economic outlook. I believe that the days of the American public's general exuberance about the future—high expectations and optimism regarding sales, profits, growth, and high share prices for corporations of all sizes—those days are over. Now households, corporations, and even the government face a future that is uncertain and less optimistic than before. People now understand that the future really depends upon hard assets rather than paper assets. At the same time, both corporations and households have accumulated huge amounts of debt due to easy credit. This debt may soon prohibit them from additional spending. As they spend less and save more, sales and profits decline. Therefore, corporate expectations about the future become less optimistic week after week.

Until a few months ago, we were expecting that the Federal Reserve would stimulate more spending in the economy by cutting interest rates and extending credit. However, the ability of the Fed to stimulate spending is limited nowadays because households face a bleak future with growing unemployment, reduced earnings, and a heavy load of debt to pay. The Fed has only the ability to affect short-term interest rates.

On the other hand, long-term interest rates, which affect the economic future, are determined by the bond markets. Those markets in turn are influenced by the expectations of the people. The Fed can only indirectly affect the prime rate as well as long-term interest rates of debt securities, such as promissory notes, bonds, and low-grade securities of any maturity. Because bondholders perceive that risk has increased, risk valuations have been upgraded in the last several months. In addition, we observe a shortage of government bonds caused by the Treasury Department's efforts to reduce the public debt. This has caused the spreads between interest rates on government securities and those on lower-grade bonds to escalate. As those spreads widen, the ability of corporations to raise capital decreases. Thus, we may be driven into a credit crunch that might become the first step toward an economic slump.

If we doubt that the Fed has been losing its ability to affect the markets by manipulating interest rates, we should consider Japan. The Bank of Japan has kept short-term interest rates at almost zero level for several years without stimulating the Japanese economy. A central bank's ability to affect markets is limited when the economy faces a pessimistic and uncertain future.

Some may say that the same kind of problem existed in the 1930s, but I don't think that we will see a repetition of the 1930s. Fortunately, we are not suffering from a deflationary recession right now, and the Fed is trying to keep that possibility away from the United States (The Bank of Japan was not able to do it, and the Japanese economy has fallen into a deflationary slump.) The greatest challenge for the Fed, rather than the manipulation of interest rates, now lies in the following three areas: (1) preventing a deflationary recession from taking place, (2) creating a climate of optimism and positive anticipation regarding the future by taking unanticipated actions, (3) ensuring that the international economy establishes an anchor.

The inability of the Fed to influence the future is demonstrated by the fact that its actions are routinely anticipated and built into long-term interest rates. Even before the Fed moves, investors anticipate when it will cut interest rates by at least another one hundred base points. Everyone expects the Fed to continue lowering aggressively in the future. Since this has already been built into their expectations, such actions by the Fed have no effect in the economy. The element of surprise has been taken out of the picture. Only unanticipated actions by the Fed will be able to stimulate the economy and have any effect. As long as actions by the Fed are anticipated and discounted in advance, the Fed's ability to influence the economy is very limited.

Taxes and the Economy

If the Fed cannot stimulate the economy, could a fiscal stimulus like cutting taxes help? Unfortunately, the answer is no. It takes much longer for tax cuts to be digested by the markets, and,more importantly, the equity markets do not want tax cuts so much as a spending stimulus and an optimistic business climate. A tax cut can neither produce a spending stimulus nor create an optimistic climate. Tax cuts are designed nowadays primarily to stimulate savings rather than spending, and what the economy needs right now is spending rather than savings.

We always need to remember that one of the major causes of a slowdown is insufficient spending, insufficient demand. With tax cuts designed primarily to stimulate savings, they do not help the economy. Actually, a tax cut may hurt the economy by postponing spending and therefore guiding the economy into a deflationary scenario. The markets need unanticipated stimulus. So the challenge for the Federal government and the Federal Reserve is to design policies that are not expected by the markets and have not already been built into investors' expectations—policies that have not already been discounted in the minds, actions, and programs of households and corporations.

Where Do We Invest?

How do we act, plan, and invest in response to all of these things? This is a question that a retired person might have, as well as a thirty-year-old or any individual or household that has some interest in the stock market. I believe we need to think strategically. We know one thing—interest rates are coming down. Therefore, strategic thinking requires us to identify industries that will benefit from the current economic climate, as well as corporations that will benefit from lower interest rates. Those industries are health care, financial networks, energy companies, and some selected retail and technology companies. In the upcoming months, we should be very cautious about designing a strategy that will guarantee some income and exploit the growth opportunities that exist because of the current economic climate. So the careful investor will think not only of industries and corporations that will benefit from lower interest rates, but also of corporations that can provide an assured income (i.e., corporations that traditionally have paid good dividends.)

I recommend that investors restructure their portfolios in such a way that they have some kind of guaranteed income from dividends. This might be considered a contrarian strategy. However, remember that just four months ago, the consensus was the corporate earnings would grow by 29 percent in the final three months of 2000. The consensus dropped to 14 percent by early December, and to just 3 percent in January of 2001. Growth stocks fell from a cliff and no one knows where the bottom is.

The heavy overinvestment that took place in the telecommunication industry and other technology-oriented industries has been hit especially hard. The investment growth rate in those industries has now declined from 28 percent to 3 percent growth rate. We see the same in the semiconductor industry, where sales growth has fallen from 35 percent to barely 9 percent. Generally speaking, the growth of capital spending on behalf of corporations has slowed down from 25 percent to barely 10 percent. Earnings across the sector of the S&P 500 are estimated to be between 7 and 8 percent this year. Therefore, an investment portfolio that would return between 7 and 10 percent would be considered pretty good for the year 2001.

Specific Investment Recommendations

Because I advocate a cautious investment strategy, I would recommend that an individual investor examine the price/earnings

(P/E) ratio of any corporations included in a portfolio. Given that the P/E ratio in the market right now is around 23 or 24, I believe you should compare the P/E ratio of your technology or blue chip stock to that range. I do not mean that you should avoid a company whose P/E exceeds 23 or 24. Some companies have a bright future and ought sell at a premium. However, I doubt that such companies can be found in the technology sector; at least it is very difficult to find them there. Rather I look for such industries outside of technology, such as in medical devices.

Speaking of the technology sector, a strategic move would be to shift your technology investments into a proven mutual fund. One such fund would be the First Hand Technology value fund, which has had a stellar performance in the last five years. While most technology funds lost significant ground in the past year, the performance of First Hand was not that bad. It lost only about 9 percent when most technology funds lost at least 25–30 percent. Again, I would emphasize strategic thinking. Identify companies that have proven they can grow even when the economy slows. They should have experience and expertise, with management teams that can remain focused on goals that benefit both the corporation and its shareholders. Focus on corporations that have increased their earnings capacity for the last decade. Strategic thinking requires you to divest companies that have weak cash flows or big debt-equity ratios.

You should also incorporate some demographic trends into this stock evaluation. Those trends reveal that as the population ages some health care companies will enjoy rising profits. History shows that pharmaceutical and medical-devices companies enjoy higher profits and growth in a climate of low interest rates, so I would be looking for companies that have good profit margins and, low competition and are able to patent either drugs or medical devices that will give them some kind of monopoly in the market. I can immediately think of two companies that have the above characteristics: Abbott Laboratories and Medtronic. Abbott has strong new products in the pipeline. It is not only a powerful pharmaceutical company, but also a company that has proven that it can grow in a climate with recession and economic slowdown. Abbott's proven record as a leader in medical devices and nutritional products makes it one of the best candidates for high growth for the next three years. Additionally, the company's earnings and dividends have grown at double-digit rates for the past decade.

I previously mentioned the need to concentrate on companies that have a rich cash flow and thing strategically about the future. Both Abbott and Medtronic qualify. They have a rich cash flow and research and development budgets that exceed a billion dollars a year. This is enough to maintain a good stream of new products, which will have patents for fourteen years. Medtronic is developing a medical device that would allow doctors to monitor the vital signs of patients who are at home. This patent will drive Medtronic to very good growth in the next several years. Despite the fact that Medtronic sells at a premium right now, I believe that it is a good company to have in an investment portfolio in this economic climate.

Another industry that benefits in a climate of low interest rates and economic slowdown is the financial industry. One company in this sector is American International Group (AIG), which has proven that it can generate good profit in almost any economic climate, but especially in a slowdown. It has strategically positioned itself all around the world, especially in markets that are not experiencing economic slowdown. Its global position, its ability to generate 20 percent annual earnings year after year, and its ability to maneuver assets profitably, make me consider owning AIG a strategic move. AIG's balance sheet includes a massive bond portfolio, and the returns from lower interest rates should be tremendous. The fact that it is positioning itself in countries where people have just started discovering the advantages of insurance, and the fact that retiring baby-boomers in the United States will need additional coverage, give this company unusual strength that cannot be found in other companies in the financial field for the next 5–6 years.

A third sector that could benefit from an economic slowdown is the energy sector. Several energy companies have excellent management, good prospects, double-digit earnings, and bright prospects. As I observe the energy sector, I can identifiy one company that has proven itself a global leader. Emerson Electric has a corporate memory that stretches back 110 years, demonstrating the company's ability to avoid cycles of boom and bust. Over the last fifty years, Emerson Electric was able to report forty-three years of uninterrupted earnings growth and a composite rate of 11 percent annually. The company sailed through the recessions of 1974, 1980–1981, 1990–1991 without negative impact. Its dividend has risen at an annual compound rate of 12 percent. If we look at the stock market for 2000, we see that Emerson's shares have traveled in exactly the opposite way from the dot-coms.

Another factor to keep in mind in portfolio and asset allocation is the need to consider taxes. Municipal bonds might be a safe place to park funds in this climate. A 10–20 percent municipal bond allocation has the following advantages:

1.) It lowers the portfolio's volatility and exposure to risk. Recent studies have shown that you only sacrifice less than half a percent return if you have 10–20 percent in a bond market versus having it in the stock market. However, the risk and volatility of the portfolio is reduced by a significant 14 percent. Therefore, having 10–20 percent of your portfolio in municipal bonds reduces risk significantly.

2.) The tax efficiency of that allocation is also significant, especially for individuals who are in the 28 percent federal tax bracket. You don't have to pay taxes on the fixed income of tax-exempt municipal bonds.

Conclusion

Let me close by saying that there are thousands of stocks available. We could spend several more pages debating the particular merits of investing in a specific industry or stock. However, we should always focus on the larger picture of how the economy operates.

When we judge an economy's prospects, we do not need to look at the growth rate of the GDP. We do not need to look at the inflation rate. We don't even need to look at the budget surplus or the level of the stock market. The only thing that we need to focus on is the economy's ability to produce more at a lower cost—i.e., the productivity growth rate.

Productivity is crucial for the stock market because it is crucial for profits. Productivity is the key for economic growth. Productivity is the key to inflation because it keeps costs down. Productivity is the key for government budget surpluses because, as corporations and households produce more at lower cost, they generate increased tax receipts for the government. Earlier I discussed whether the productivity surge of the last five years has been cyclical or structural. Despite the fact that the last report of former President Clinton claimed that virtually all of the increase of productivity since 1995 has been structural, I questioned that assumption. While we experienced average productivity growth of 1.4 percent from the 1970s until the early 1990s, we had a productivity growth rate of 3–4 percent annually in the past five years. Unfortunately, we are also experiencing a productivity slowdown to an annualized level of 2.2 percent as shown by government data released the week of February 5, 2001. Our huge current-account deficit (which has tripled in the last two years) makes me concerned about the ability of the United States to attract foreign capital to sustain output at the current level. I also question the ability of the markets and of the Fed to maintain the dollar at its current value against other currencies. How productivity holds up will depend primarily on how firms adjust their investments spending. Economic analysts used to say that investment, especially information technology investments, would be immune to an economic cycle. However, we have been discovering lately that they were wrong. Firms have cut their spending plans. Investments fell in the fourth quarter of 2000 for the first time in nine years.

A productivity slowdown will have negative implications for the current-account deficit, for the dollar, and for the prospect of the whole economy. So again, investors need to think strategically about how they view the equity markets and how they adjust their own portfolios.

On Viruses, Markets, Risks, and Visions: An Historical Perspective on Investments

Presented March 2001

Anyone who examines the U.S. and global economies would have to say that something is wrong with our global financial structure. The question, of course, is: What is wrong? In this essay, I will consider some related questions to try to determine what is ailing our economy. However, before I do so, I believe that a few words on vision are appropriate. We need to remember that the budget of an organization is not merely a list of its anticipated expenses, but also a record of its vision and its moral priorities. The budget does not reflect a list of bills to be paid, but rather a vision of what is most important to the organization and those associated with it.

In the ocean of challenges and opportunities before us, we need to remember that we cannot discover the benefits of our economic trip unless we lost sight of the shore. Departure from the known and adventure toward the unknown is essential for gaining a vision that can transform individuals and nations. Look at the story of the Hebrew patriarch Abraham. He trusted God's promise that he would become the father of nations. Reality is only for those without imagination. Thus began the adventures of the Jewish people, which continues four thousand years later. If we dare to embark on a visionary trip, we know that we will face tremendous opposition. However, faith amid these circumstances becomes a wind that fills our sails and carries us onward. People of faith dare to venture because living conventional lives is boring. God's call is an invitation to cathedral thinking that focuses on the future by laying today the foundation of a grand structure that will be enjoyed for generations to come.

In Judges 5, we find a wonderful poem that is known as the Song of Deborah. Deborah rallied the Israelites to go and acquire the land of Canaan. There were some debates, and among the tribal leaders, searching of hearts. (The tribe of Asher wanted to remain along the creeks, for example.) We see several responses to the call of Deborah to go and claim the land that the Lord had promised her people. The Lord always had been faithful to His promises.

However, sometimes our responses resemble the indecision and debate of the Israelites, some of whom (like the tribe of Gilead) chose to stay in the same place and do nothing. I am fascinated by the picture of the tribe of Asher, clinging to their creeks. In the face of the big opportunity, they chose the little. They didn't want the liberation of risk, just the security of the creek. I believe that throughout history we find creek-minded people and ocean-minded people.

In Chile is the harbor of Valparaiso, full of wrecked boats and ships. When a storm blows in from the Pacific, wise boat captains steam out of the harbor into the ocean, where they can ride out the storm. Vessels that stay in the apparent safety of the harbor are broken and wrecked. Safety can be found in the open sea, in adventure upon the deep. By engaging in the risks that God calls us to take, we allow Him to form and perfect our lives. Those who try to find security by clinging to the things they know are destined to be wrecked. We human beings are made for growth, for creation, and for action. We need to take the liberating risks that can transform our lives.

Recently, I have been reading E. Stanley Jones's works. In his autobiography and other writings, he says that a person who will not stick out his neck, for fear it will get hurt, soon will be dead because his head will have no ideas worth thinking about! Jones continues by saying that the turtle only starts going places when she sticks out her neck.

Peace in our personal and corporate lives will come as we discover the fruit of actions we take in the midst of conflict, in the midst of sorrow, in the midst of the storm. Christ said, "My peace I give unto you," at the moment when the shadow of the Cross was falling darkly upon His life mission. God had entrusted Him a mission and He was perfecting that mission. Christ found purpose in His pain; so do His followers today. So what kind of vision do we have for the economy, ourselves, and our society? Do we understand which risks could truly transform our global village if properly undertaken? Let's go to the critical questions promised you at the opening of this chapter.

Some Critical Questions

1.) Why is Federal Reserve Chairman Alan Greenspan so aggressive in his monetary easing? Is he afraid of something? Does he know something that the public does not? Is the monetary policy neutral according to the traditional measures of real interest rates? The aggressive cutting of interest rates starting on January 3, 2001, reveals the fact that the bubble created in the U.S. economy (in equities and real estate, as well as in other markets) had been supported by the Fed's monetary policy. That policy diverged from sound fiscal policy because it did not take into consideration the global dynamics of trade, currency values, production, and productivity growth rates. If we look at the traditional measures of real interest rates, we have to say with some certainty that current monetary policy is not too loose but actually neutral.

2.) Why don't the equity markets respond more positively to monetary easing? Do we understand what truly affects corporate profits? Do we understand what affects productivity? Do we understand why bankers are cutting the credit lines to corporations, possibly making them liable to default on their existing loans? We might say that when the markets do not respond to monetary easing, the Fed is dancing alone. It is peculiar to see federal institutions as well as private financial institutions refusing to respond to the Fed's monetary jazz.

3.) Why has the euphoria of the equity markets suddenly died? The boom of the 1990s created exuberant expectations (profit growth rates of 15–20%), which have now turned to uncertainty. Again we could say that corporations overbuilt their capacity in the 1990s expecting high profitability that never materialized. We have had clear signs since the third quarter of 1999 that corporate profitability is declining fast. Therefore, slowdown and recession may be hitting the country in months to come. The NASDAQ has lost more than 65 percent of its value since its record high in March of 2000.

4.) Are we dealing with some kind of global virus that has affected the financial markets? If so, how does this virus spread? Indeed, we could say that we are dealing with the virus of uncertainty. This sickness has been created by overinvestment, and it spreads via international trade. For example, Canada exports one-third of its GDP to the United States, and Mexico exports 25 percent of its GDP to the United States. Therefore, if the U.S. economy slows down, the GDP of both Canada and Mexico will fall. That will have detrimental effects throughout the western hemisphere. Is American use of informtion technolgy a factor? Yes, especially when we consider that 80 percent of Malaysia's exports to the U.S. comes form information technology. The corresponding figure for South Korea and Taiwan is 50 percent. Southeast Asian countries such as Taiwan, South Korea, Malaysia, Singapore, and Thailand depend upon exports to the United States for their growth, prosperity, and income by as much as 70–80 percent. So when the United States slows down, it has a significant effect on that region. We could have easily predicted that as the U.S. economy slowed down those economies would move into a recession. We could also have predicted the rise of economic uncertainty in Latin America, with the possible default of Argentina. Does this global slowdown have anything to do with globally integrated stock markets, which allowed the economic virus to travel fast? The answer again is yes, because the correlation among markets has risen by at least 55 percent in the last six years. Now the correlation among international equity and debt markets is as high as 65 and 70 percent.

5.) Why isn't the globalization of trade helping to offset all of this? What kind of risk-taking among global partners could liberate the economy from the slowdown? Globalization can be seen in technology transfers, in investments overseas, in capital movements (of both financial and physical capital), in people's movements, in outsourcing of production abroad, in mergers and acquisitions among global companies, in increased international trade flows, and in equity trading systems. But the thing that could liberate this global economy from its malaise is a new kind of vision. For all of its accomplishments, globalization has given us no new vision of how we should live together on this planet.

6.) Are we looking at the right macroeconomic picture? If we had been looking at the right picture, could we have foreseen the energy problem that we faced in 2000? Could we have foreseen the financial imbalances that had been created since early 1998? Could we have foreseen that the current American slowdown is primarily supply driven? The swing of the economic pendulum has been pretty unstable. We are moving quickly from one extreme to another. Such exuberance and despair creates instability and uncertainty, which contribute to trade imbalances, stock market imbalances, debt imbalances, profit uncertainties, and erratic economic cycles that undermine prosperity. The global economy is running out of energy because it lacks a wholistic economic vision.

7.) Is U.S. economic action sufficient to overcome the global difficulties, or do we need a global coordinated effort? If the United States and Japan account for 46 percent of the world's output and both of them are trapped in a liquidity crisis, is any country or group of countries able to pull us out of the trap? The introduction of the Euro in January 2002 may further undermine Europe's potential to do this. Moreover, Europe suffers from an inflexibility that does not allow European countries to change quickly or become the agents of change. If the dollar starts losing ground, the United States will lose credibility in the world's markets. That could have a significant negative effect in the global economy. The Japanese economy cannot pull us out of recession, especially with the banking problems they are facing. The United States has overbuilt its capacity, and it will take longer than anticipated to ride out the overcapacity. I am afraid that by the end of the year we are going to see unemployment rates higher than we have known since the early 1990s.[1]

A Historical Perspective on Investments

I would like to make a few points of historical review. First, there have been periods within the last 130 years when stocks under- performed other financial instruments such as bonds.

Second, the American stock market does not always recover from a sell-off within months or even within a year. Therefore, we should not necessarily expect the pendulum to swing the other way within a year.

Third, the fact that investors tend to overestimate returns and revenues and do not fully comprehend equity premiums and time and price risks creates additional market risks during a recovery. Investors have a habit of driving the instruments to unrealistically high levels without understanding that stock prices represent residual claims on corporate cash flows.

Fourth, investing in mutual funds does not necessarily minimize an investor's risk and is not always the best strategy during a recovery. This is true especially if those mutual funds are concentrated in particular sectors of the economy or in a particular region's economy.

Fifth, we need to analyze carefully why there was such a dramatic increase in the Dow Jones Industrial Average. The Dow stood at 3,600 in early 1994 and rocketed to about 11,500 by the start of 2000. Why? Did personal income in the United States increase similarly? Did corporate profits increase similarly? Did the GDP grow similarly? This is a good time to ask whether we understand the true fundamentals of the stock market.

We can clearly see from the first graph below that the so-called millennium boom was not marked by real earnings growth. The graph also shows that the sharp run-up in the market was followed by a period of flat returns and/or negative ones. It is clear from this first figure that while earnings increased in the 1990s by less than 10 percent per year, the stock market valuation increased by many times that amount.[2]

Real S&P Composite Stock Price Index   Real S&P Composite earnings

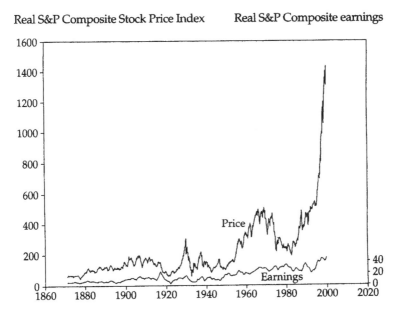

SOURCE: Schiller, R.J.: *Irrational Exuberance.* Copyright © 2000 by Princeton University Press. Reprinted by permission of Princeton University Press.

The graph of the price/earnings ratio shows three major spikes, in 1901, 1929, and 1966. All of those spikes were followed by significant if not dramatic declines in stock value. The P/E trend appears to have power over what will happen to the equities market. Unfortunately, the recent P/E trend suggests an impending stock sell-off.

Price-earnings ratio

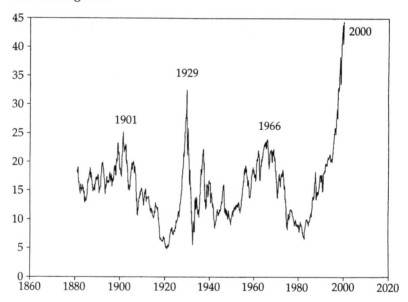

SOURCE: Schiller, R.J.: *Irrational Exuberance.* Copyright © 2000 by Princeton University Press. Reprinted by permission of Princeton University Press.

The third graph has important lessons for us also. For years when stocks' P/E ratio was very high, those same stocks' returns for the following years have been very low or negative. On the other hand, years with low P/E ratios have been followed by high returns. Note that this kind of relationship holds true for the economies of entire countries as well as for individual stocks.

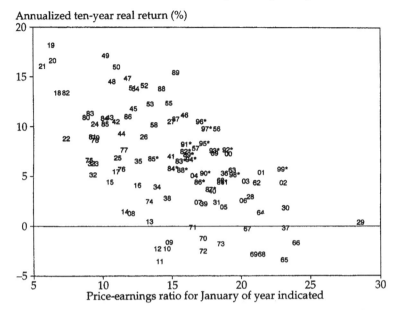

SOURCE: Schiller, R.J.: *Irrational Exuberance.* Copyright © 2000 by Princeton University Press. Reprinted by permission of Princeton University Press.

Our next point in this historical review is that we have not learned the right lessons from the dividend yield. History teaches us that, under normal circumstances, times of low dividends relative to stock prices tend to be followed by price decline and stock market sell-offs. Therefore, when an investor does not receive increasing dividends as a percentage of the price paid for the stock, that is an indication to stop buying that stock. Given the fact that dividends have been poor, especially from 1997 to 1999, we had a clear indication that the stock market was due for a significant decline.

Now someone could obviously ask, "Why did the market experience this bubble?" I believe we can identify six primary reasons for the dynamics of the markets in the last few years. We need to remember that only fundamental factors such as the growth of earnings, the change of real interest rates, and the rate of change in productivity can change stock valuations. Only these real fundamental factors affect the true underlying value of stocks.

However, the following six factors that are not related to the fundamentals have contributed to the bubble:

1.) The arrival of exciting new technologies that coincided with good investment earnings reports, although these new technologies had little to do with those earnings.

2.) Increased media coverage of investment and economic news, which created an artificial demand for equities, coupled with analysts' overly optimistic reports.

3.) Analysts' increasingly optimistic forecasts regarding the future, which created unrealistic expectations in investment circles.

4.) A proliferation of pension plans, 401K plans, and mutual funds, which created an artificial demand for stocks that had nothing to do with the fundamental value of those stocks.

5.) The rise of e-traders and twenty-four-hour trading, which created an unstable environment that increased stock portfolio turnover from 40 percent to over 80 percent annually in the last fifteen years.

6.) A misunderstanding of risk and a significant increase in the gambling culture, which transformed investment decisions into casino decisions.

Market uncertainty brings market instability, which feeds confusion. This pattern signifies a lack of economic vision and a loss of investment focus for individuals, families, corporations, institutions, and nations.

The Charms of the Market, the Sunset of "The Madness of the People," and the Dollar

Presented May 2001

S ir Isaac Newton once commented, "I can calculate the motions of the heavenly bodies but not the madness of the people." He had just lost heavily by trading in the market. On June 4, 1864, Karl Marx wrote to his good friend Friedrich Engels that he had "made a killing on the Stock Exchange here. The time has come again when, with wit and very little money, it's possible to make money in London." A couple of years earlier he had commented to another friend in Germany, "I have been speculating partly in American funds, but more especially in English stocks which are springing up like mushrooms this year…are forced up to quite an unreasonable level and then, for the most part collapse."

The charms of the market lured even the most influential critic of capitalism into what he described as a mere speculation. The motions and swings of the market were seen as mere madness by the genius Sir Isaac Newton.

Friends inevitably ask, "When will stock prices stop falling? Have we seen the bottom yet? Is the recovery here?"

I like to reverse the question by asking: "Are we ready to take that bait?" The prominent economist Jeremy Siegel wrote in his book *Stocks for the Long Run* that stocks are the best long-term investment one can make. Furthermore, as a proponent of the New Economy, Siegel claims that the historical price earnings (P/E) ratio of about 15 is obsolete. He argues that because the twentieth-century record included such events as the Great Depression, prolonged recessions, two world wars, double-digit inflation, and high interest rates, all of those need to be taken out of the P/E calculations. He suggests that without discounting those events (which he believes cannot happen again), the historical P/E ratio is understated. Thus the current higher P/E ratio is justified.

My contention is that the historical averages cannot be neglected, because they reflect central tendencies of a market that always will experience dispersion due to the unpredictability of human action. We are moving into an era when people will rediscover the meaning of savings, when real wealth may again be created, and when the speculative "madness of the people" might end.

However, before we look at some economic history, allow me please to refer to Nehemiah 2:17: "You see the trouble we are in: Jerusalem lies in ruins, and its gates have been burned with fire. Come, let us rebuild the wall of Jerusalem, and we will no longer be in disgrace." The once-prominent city of Jerusalem had lay in ruins for many years. Then the Jews got a fresh vision of rebuilding their beloved city. In our lives too, after devastating things have taken place, a rebuilding time must come. That is a time when we concentrate our efforts in starting anew. In the economic sphere, markets correct and sometimes collapse. After a fair assessment, the rebuilding process starts with concentrated and collective efforts that focus on one thing—how to make the city stronger, avoiding both speculative bubbles and the escape mentality.

We cannot escape our situation. We need to face reality as it is. We need to take our situation, even when it is in ruins, and make something out of it. We need to transform our ruins and experience metamorphosis. In the process of our own metamorphosis, we will become agents of transformation. We can transform injustice into justice, pain into pleasure. We can look at the example of Christ, who took some uneducated fishermen and made them teachers. Jesus transformed everything He touched. This is also our task: metamorphosis and rebuilding.

Having said that, let's go back to Jeremy Siegel's argument about accelerating P/E ratios. If Siegel were right, we should exclude not only the bad times from our historical calculations but also some good times too. Examples would be the run-up of the market in the 1920s, the bull market of the 1950s and 1960s, and, of course, the bull market of the 1990s.

There are indeed some positive influences at work in today's economy, such as breakthroughs in technology, advances in global trade and finance, and better understanding of economic dynamics. However, we also need to take into account similar advances that have occurred before. Thinking that we live in a new era is symptomatic of the false prosperity of our day.

The rise in productivity that we saw in the last three to four years is primarily cyclical rather than structural. This is proven by fact that as the economy started slowing down, so did the rate of productivity growth.

The 1920s were also a time of widespread technological advances. In 1914, there were only 1.7 million registered cars. By 1920, there were over 8 million and by 1929, over 23 million! In 1920, there were only three radio stations in the United States, but by 1923, there were more than five hundred. Exuberance generated by the over-optimism of that "new era" created a stock-market fervor that deceived even famous economists of that era such as Irving Fisher. Trusting that manipulative monetary policy could fine tune the economy led in the 1960s to the overextension of credit and to the corporate mess of the 1970s.

Therefore, the heralded innovations of this "new era" are not unique. Even the celebrated expansion of global trade and finance has been seen before, and we have experienced the bitter taste of those results.

The bubble that was created in the 1990s through the expansion of monetary aggregates and the easing of credit conditions has many similarities to the historical bubbles of previous centuries. The tulip mania of 1636–1637 and the European trading bubble of 1719–1720 resemble today's situation in several ways:

1.) There was a government-sponsored attempt to shift investments away from hard assets and into equities. (Does this teach us anything about the current effort on Capitol Hill to move Social Security funds to Wall Street investments?)

2.) The management of the companies involved had a vested interest in cooking the books to inflate profits, hide costs, and push share prices to higher levels. Furthermore, the potential future earnings of those companies were exaggerated on the assumption that new technologies would give them monopolistic positions in their markets (Does this remind us of the Internet bubble?)

3.) Monetary easing overextended credit and inflated the speculative bubble.

4.) As new technologies created a euphoria of optimism and over-investment, speculators built excess manufacturing capacity. Moreover, a general feeling prevailed that a new era had finally arrived with unprecedented and unstoppable growth opportunities.

5.) Foreign investment money found a desirable place to be parked, since the London market was considered a safe haven.

6.) Neighboring markets (e.g., the one in Paris) suffered as capital was shifted to speculation. (Does this teach us anything about today's situation with Latin America, where serious problems in Argentina's debt may bring down both Argentina and Brazil, not to mention Mexico and Chile?)

7.) The economy was characterized by commercial expansion and colonization of the overseas market (read globalization).

An Update on the Economy: The Road Ahead

Conventional wisdom now says that the following factors have contributed to the economic slowdown:

1.) The manufacturing sector was already in recession; thus, it feels like the whole economy is in a recession.

2.) High-tech industries are registering negative growth numbers, but this is merely an aberration of their start-up period.

3.) The Fed raised interest rates in 2000 in order to keep the economy from overheating, but that unduly raised the cost of doing business.

4.) After the stock market dropped, consumption fell. Profit expectations then declined, making it harder for companies to raise capital.

5.) Higher energy costs have created a budget crunch for both businesses and households.

6.) Inventory build-up has forced businesses to slow down their investments and to lay off people. But this will change as soon as public confidence is restored.

The road ahead is not as rosy as some analysts want us to believe. Here's why:

1.) We have created a supply overhang by overbuilding our excess capacity. Now businesses do not want to spend on capital improvements because they overspent in the last four to five years, and then saw such spending did not pay off.

2.) The market has started discounting the Fed's reduction in the interest rate. Lowering interest rates has thus become a questionable device for revitalizing the economy. It did not work in Japan, so it may not work in the United States either.

3.) The yield of long-term debt securities has started rising. This indicates both higher borrowing costs and fears of inflation.

4.) Similar periods of boom in the past have been followed by periods of bust that lasted longer than the one-year downturn we anticipate now.

5.) The increasing unemployment rate will contribute to greater pessimism.

6.) The global slowdown—especially as it is observed in Europe and Japan—will ripple back to the United States through declining exports. This will cause further deterioration of our balance of payments with other nations.

7.) We have overtrusted the equities market to guide our economies. Thus, we have placed so much emphasis on forecasting stock prices that we have almost forgotten that they are nothing but the product of investors' opinions, which are subjective.

8.) The Fed's tinkering with the markets misallocates resources and creates inefficiencies that water the seeds of another economic bust.

9.) Bad news from the corporate world will keep on coming. Nortel's announced loss of $19.2 billion was the second-biggest quarterly corporate loss ever. If we try to justify it by saying it was due to write-offs of acquisitions that Nortel made, we should also consider future write-offs by companies like Cisco (with forty-five acquisition takeovers in the last five years), Lucent, Sun, and others. Can we imagine what will follow?

10.) The dollar is overvalued and its future decline to more realistic levels will trigger a sequence of events that will undermine any growth prospect. The dollar's real trade-weighted exchange value against fifty-five developed and emerging-market currencies is at a sixteen-year high. Until last year that could have been justified by the high-flying economy due to capital inflows from abroad, but that's no longer true. Currency movements can be explained in three primary ways: growth rates and prospects; bond-yield differentials; and net equity portfolio flows. On this basis, the dollar should have already fallen this year. American economic growth has slowed significantly relative to Europe. The bond differentials have been eliminated since the Fed has been reducing the interest rates, that is the return on the bonds. The United States still attracts some foreign investors to her capital markets; however, foreign direct investments have slowed down. More important, the United States current-account imbalances are not sustainable. This imbalance inevitably will force the value of the dollar down. The weaker dollar will force greater equity portfolio liquidations, increase the cost of living, and increase the borrowing costs of corporations. All of these consequences will cause the deterioration of growth prospects of the American economy.

Mortgaging Our Economic Future

Presented August 2001

In previous chapters, we had the opportunity to explore the direction of the markets and, to some extent, predict the direction of the macroeconomy. Unfortunately, as 2001 has progressed, we have to admit that the overall evaluation was right. The economy has been slowing down dramatically. We have been observing a profit recession and a dramatic cutback in investments—i.e., a drop in capital spending. This slowdown had led the manufacturing sector into a recession. The bursting of the bubble, especially in the NASDAQ index, leads to the suspicion that a significant slowdown in consumer confidence—with a corresponding increase in the unemployment rate and a cutback in spending—may be approaching.

In addition, in the previous chapter we projected a fall in the dollar's value. This has now started taking place. We also hinted that another bubble had been created in the housing sector.

The focus of this chapter will be threefold. First, I would like to elaborate on this housing bubble, which indeed mortgages our future. Second, I would like to explore the direction of the global economy and the upcoming global recession. Third, I would like us to think critically about our personal and corporate investment policies for the months to come. However, before we start exploring these issues, allow me to share the following devotional thoughts.

In 1 Corinthians 1:27–29, Paul writes: "But God chose the foolish things of the world to shame the wise; God chose the weak thinks of the world to shame the strong. He chose the lowly things of this world and the despised things—and the things that are not—to nullify the things that are, so that no one may boast before him." All of us have a place that we call home. We take care of it not only because it represents an asset but also because we have an emotional attachment to it. Christ also spoke of the place that He went to prepare for us (John 14). We must admit that a Christian's mind sometimes is inflated with cheap intellectualism that prevents God's Spirit from completing the work of grace. We may feel that we are in charge of things and that we are making a difference. In those moments, we unfortunately domesticate the gospel and create a god in our own image, perfectly fitted into our own values and priorities. Thus, we convert our churches into social alternatives that require no commitments or sacrifices from their members. We have let the world determine our questions, and thus we have limited our answers to those that respond to those questions. I fear that sometimes we as God's people have lost the countercultural way of doing God's business and have found it convenient to do our business in our way in God's house (Mark 11:15–17). I only hope that this distortion of the gospel soon will end.

The Housing Bubble

Historically speaking, economic bubbles have dual manifestations. If we look back in the nineteenth century, we see that the Industrial Revolution and the new technologies of oil exploration created the dual bubble of railroad speculation and massive consumer spending. The forces that drove prosperity in the late nineteenth century—such as the burgeoning railroad industry, the telegraph system, immigration, and industrialization—led to an exuberant spirit. This evolved into the overbuilding of industrial capacity. At the same time, the tycoons of the day lived in wretched excess, which common people imitated in over-consumption.

In the twentieth century, we saw a similar kind of exuberance in the 1920s that led to overconsumption, overbuilding, and overinvestment. All of these created excess capacities in the major sectors of the economy. We saw excesses in the 1920s, 1950s, and 1960s in the real estate sector and the manufacturing sector. We seem not to have learned from the economic lessons of the last 150 years.

The bubble that the United States economy experienced in the 1990s was created by exuberance in the information technology sector, over-investment in capital spending, globalization, and perceived higher capacity to produce. We have not fully comprehended that this bubble has an equity dimension, a housing dimension, and a dollar value dimension. To a large extent devaluation of the dollar is a fruit of the excesses in the equities market. Due to the fact that U.S. investments had been experiencing high rates of return, foreign capital was attracted to the U.S. markets beginning in the mid-1990s. Therefore, the value of the dollar increased. When the U.S. markets decline, one can easily conclude, that the U.S. dollar will decline, too.

Now let us consider the housing dimension of the 1990s economic bubble. While NASDAQ is off by about 30 percent since the beginning of the year and overall stock prices are down by about 14 percent, housing prices keep rising at an annual rate of 8 to 10 percent. Investors have begun shifting their investments into real estate. Unfortunately, the Federal Reserve seems to encourage this by its dramatic rate-cutting campaign to revitalize the economy. It's obvious that the Fed has not learned its lesson. The Fed cannot affect the long-term interest rates that really matter and can only give some direction in the short-term interest rates that really do not matter. In today's global economy, markets determine interest rates. Therefore, the economy cannot be revitalized through a rate-cutting campaign by a central bank.

Economists often speak about the "wealth effect": Individuals experienced significant increases in their net worth due to the rising stock market in the 1990s and felt they could spend more because of that perceived higher net worth. This was another misconception of the 1990s. The most important investment of the average household is the investment in their home. Unfortunately, in the last several months we have seen individuals mortgaging their homes in order to sustain the unrealistic consumption levels that the exuberant economy encouraged. It will take a far smaller drop in property values than in the stock market to deliver a devastating blow to the economy.

Financial institutions would be badly hurt by such a decline of property values because pseudogovernment agencies securitize mortgages. This process has resulted in the building up of excess credit. Personal bankruptcies are already on the rise and the unemployment rate keeps increasing. Therefore, if home prices fall, many homeowners will not make their mortgage payment due to the level of debt they have acquired. More specifically, if the housing bubble bursts, the net worth of families will be reduced significantly. Consumption will suffer dramatically. Financial institutions will be devastated. This scenario, coupled with the falling dollar, could produce catastrophic consequences.

Since the time of my prior presentation, when I predicted the fall of the dollar, the dollar has lost 11 percent of its value against the Euro. The falling dollar will undermine equities as well as the debt markets and will halt foreign capital flows.

Corporate investments are made in an environment of stability and growth. Stability and growth cannot take place if there is overbuilt capacity, overextension of credit, and the heavy debt burden that hangs over American corporations. In 1995, the face value of distressed debt in the United States was about $130 billion. By 1998, it had dropped to about $100 billion. By 1999, it had rebounded to the level of $300 billion. In the year 2000, it exceeded $600 billion. In the first quarter of 2001, it has already reached $600 billion. This is a scenario of instability rather than stability, and low interest rates do not help in this picture.

Several other common fiscal practices do not help. For example, we need to stop the overextension of credit in the housing market. As banks issue more questionable loans, their exposure to default increases significantly. At the beginning of the second quarter of this year, approximately $5.3 trillion of outstanding mortgage debt existed in the United States. The four biggest lenders nearly tripled their mortgage originations in the first six months of 2001. If defaults start piling up, financial institutions will be hit hard just as they were in the late 1980s and the early 1990s with the S&L crisis, which cost taxpayers more than $250 billion.

Most banks today sell off their loans to government-sponsored institutions such as Fannie Mae and Freddie Mac, which package those loans as mortgage-backed securities. Those securities are actively traded on Wall Street among corporations, foreign investors, insurance companies, and pension funds. In the year 2000 alone, more than $3 trillion worth of mortgage-backed securities were outstanding. Because of loan defaults, Fannie Mae and Freddie Mac have started to send non-performing loans back to the banks that originally made them. The debt-equity ratio of these organizations has increased by more than 50 percent in the last three years, which is unsustainable. If banks are forced to eat more of their mortgage losses, they will get scared. As the losses start piling up, financial institutions will experience tremendous stress.

Putting our hopes in the Fed is a wrong move. As we have clearly seen, the long-term effect of the Fed's actions are insignificant. As an example, few people recall Alan Greenspan's warning about irrational exuberance of five years ago. When the Federal Reserve started lowering interest rates at the beginning of this year, the stock market experienced an increase for about a month. As of today, however, the market has experienced a significant decrease. The truth is that the Fed is designed to influence the behavior of banks. However, banks no longer determine interest rates. Interest rates are determined by the bond market, not by banks. We live in a market-dominated world, and right now we have no road map to tell us what role the Fed can have in such a marketplace.

The news media suggest that minor changes in interest rates and liquidity will decide our economic growth rate by virtue of their effect on the behavior of banks. That is certainly not the case. In today's world, the Fed is only one of the players in the theatre of economic change. We need a new financial infrastructure, started with a solid foundation. That foundation will be the catharsis of the current system. Unless catharsis takes place in the telecomm sector, in information technology, in capital spending, in excess capacities, as well as in the banking and real estate sectors, the foundation for a new infrastructure will not be there. A catharsis has already begun in the housing sector: we see that the U. S. inventory of unsold homes has risen by almost 25 percent since the beginning of the year—a clear sign of overbuilt capacity. Inflated home prices and rising consumer debt have always led to a drop in home prices. We see it demonstrated in the falling prices of homes in Silicon Valley over the past ten months. The housing bubble is already bursting there.

Consumers can leverage and mortgage their net worth on assets that can easily deflate in value. That is a recipe for disaster. The fact that Freddie Mac and Fannie Mae securitize approximately two-thirds of U.S. debt and that they have jointly become the largest borrower—even bigger than the U.S. government—is clearly a sign that catharsis is needed in the housing market. Those two organizations do not have the capital reserves that private banks are required to have. Moreover, the economy relies too much on the housing sector, which by all standards is overvalued. Clearly, we have not seen the bottom yet.

An Assessment of the Global Economy

Countries such as Singapore, Mexico, Taiwan, Argentina, and Germany have either stagnated or are already in a recession. European economies are experiencing a zero growth rate. Japan's economy is in a steep decline, while many economies in Southeast Asia and Latin America are also experiencing zero or negative growth.

The striking thing about this global economic weakness is that it is more widespread than previous downturns. Globalization has made economies more integrated through trade, investment, capital flows, and technology transfers. The downside of this globalization process is magnified after the initial fall in investment demand during an economic slowdown around the globe. As foreign investments are collapsing in the United States and Japan, imports from Southeast Asian and Latin American countries are dropping significantly. That has led countries such as Singapore, Taiwan, Thailand, Mexico, and Malaysia to experience a recession.

In previous global downturns, long-term bond yields dropped, which led to economic revival. However, this time long-term bond yields have not been dropping, which is another sign of the inefficiency of the Fed, and of the need for catharsis and a new economic foundation. The motto of the global game has become "United We Fall." Clearly, we have seen significant swings in global industrial production. GDP growth rates are either negative or zero among countries and regions such as the United States, Japan, emerging East Asia, Latin America, and emerging Europe. The only exception is China.[3] Notice several factors that characterize this "United We Fall" crisis:

A. We observe higher yields on government bonds around the globe and especially in emerging markets. That's not only the sign of a credit crunch, but a desperate cry for help.

B. Foreign reserves have been dropping. That's a clear sign that currency instability may be growing.

C. Foreign debt as a percentage of GDP and as a percentage of exports in those countries and regions, has been increasing.

D. Governments have been failing consistently to find sufficient numbers of buyers at their auctions of domestic debt.

E. Country after country experiences trouble in implementing plans to revitalize its economy.

F. Stock markets around the globe are falling.

G. Growth-rate forecasts have been revised downward quarter after quarter.

H. Higher leverage for households, corporations, and nations undermines economic stability.

I. Absence of a leading economy to which problems can be exported is a major problem.

J. The strong channels of communication that globalization has established are used most often to spread panic.

K. Governments have growing difficulty in meeting their budgets.

L. Fund managers rebalance their portfolios for better performance, further depressing the value of troubled securities.

The conclusion is that there is a fundamental problem in the global economy for the first time in several decades. So what should we do? Here are several recommendations for the individual investor:

A. Allocate at least 30 percent of your portfolio to a money market account.

B. Identify areas of diversification and in those identify areas with potential growth, such as the energy sector and the health care sector.

C. Diversify outside of the United States in non-dollar-denominated investments (e.g., Euro).

D. Allocate at least 25–30 percent of your portfolio to non-dollar-denominated debt securities.

E. For the portion of your portfolio that is still in equities, go with index funds. Moreover, I recommend that you diversify your stock holdings outside the United States through index funds in various countries.

F. Discount the existing price/earnings ratios. Concentrate on indexes or debt instruments that have at least a 20 percent discount from the overall market averages.

G. Concentrate on blue chips rather than high-flying growth stocks. Moreover, concentrate on blue chips that pay consistently stable dividends.

H. Irrespective of whether a particular sector of the economy (e.g., information technology) is suffering a significant fall, it may still have stocks or financial instruments that promise a good potential. However, a word of caution is needed. The P/E ratio should be at least 10 percent less than the industry average in order for you to invest, and the dividend yield of that particular company should be at least 15 percent higher than the average dividend yield of its sector.

I. Understand what you invest in. If you do not understand the company, the products it produces, the policies it follows, and its growth prospects, do not invest in it. Exercise due diligence. Call the company and ask its investor relations department about company revenues, profit margins, costs, outlook, new products, funds that are committed to research, what the trends in the industry are, and so on.

J. Experience the thrill of bottom-fishing for bargain stocks. Consult with a financial advisor to identify companies that are in traditionally good sectors and whose fundamentals are strong, but that are temporarily experiencing problems.

Try to identify turnaround candidates. Consult with an investment expert or do your own research to identify companies that sell well below the value of their assets.

From Fear to Courage:
Lessons in an Era of Uncertainty

Presented October 2001

The days after the terrorist attacks of September 11, 2001, truly mark a new era. This new era is characterized by fear. As we look at history and compare the stages that other great nations have gone through, we understand that these days could make or break not only our economic growth process, but our nation itself.

The ultimate outcome depends upon our response to the uncertainty that these events have created. Economic history teaches us that nations and organizations that have made a mark in history are those with a contrarian mentality, a mind-set and a spirit that goes against the majority, and which is pursued with passion in a radical way.

So what is the contrarian spirit that could mark us as the visionaries who transformed everything in this new period of our history? It is the spirit of courage and risk. Courage is fear that has said its prayers. Risk is the calculated evaluation of uncertainty that liberates us from our fears.

The Story of Eddie Rickenbacker

What do these three men have in common:

…the auto racer who set the world speed record at Daytona in 1914,

…the pilot who recorded the highest number of victories in aerial combat against the Germans in World War I,

…the secretary of war's special adviser who survived a plane crash and twenty-two days on a raft in the Pacific during World War II?

All of them survived and triumphed through tough circumstances, and they all happen to be the same person—Eddie Rickenbacker.

Meeting a challenge was never a problem for Eddie Rickenbacker. When he was twelve, his father died, and he quit school to become the family's breadwinner. He worked in factories. He sold papers and eggs. As a teenager, he worked as a mechanic and then started racing. Two years later, he set the world speed record.

In the first years of World War I, he tried to enlist as an aviator. Since he was overage and undereducated, he was rejected. Instead he became a military chauffeur and persuaded his superior to send him to aviation school, where he excelled as a pilot. By the time the war was over, he had logged three hundred combat hours (the most of any American pilot), survived 134 aerial encounters, and earned the Medal of Honor, eight Distinguished Service Crosses, and the French Legion of Honor. In 1933, he became the vice president of Eastern Airlines. His leadership took Eastern through the tough times of the Depression. Within two years, he made Eastern profitable without government subsidies. His son William wrote that his father's motto was, "I will fight like a wildcat."

One thing stands out in time of crisis: the willingness to risk. Risk taking in such an environment becomes contagious and inspires others. Desire for calculated risk liberates enterprises, uplifts noble causes, and underwrites great causes. In times like these, our fear should not be that we have reached the end of an era but rather that we are failing to prepare for the next one. The success of great companies and nations lies in the fact that they view life as a kind of escalator, constantly moving. Empires fall, corporations and nations go bankrupt because they fail to change, often because they are too rigid and sclerotic to recognize that a new era is unfolding in front of them.

A Truly New Era

As a professional economist, I have read with amusement the articles that have celebrated the arrival of the "New Era." The writers had concluded that the arrival of the Internet age and the increased forces of globalization have made a permanent mark on our productivity, and thus we have reached a level where permanent growth will be sustained—we have entered an era of economic certainty.

If only we could learn that growth is achieved in an environment of calculated risk, where institutions and economic dynamics continually change, real production takes place, money is not cheapened through manipulative efforts, and people are stakeholders in the process of change. I have written and lectured extensively on the recent economic bubble that has burst. That "New Era" is over, but another new one is dawning upon us. In order for us to become participants in this newest era, the following personal attributes are needed:

A. A courage to take calculated risks that liberate us from the bondage of conventional thinking

B. A truly global perspective on issues that matter

C. An understanding of the institutions involved in the area in which to invest

D. A macroperspective of national and international economic events

E. A fundamental economic analysis of the variables involved in each particular case

F. A sense of timing as to when to make a move

My hope is that in this new era people will no longer be complacent. They will examine carefully whether a particular sector is overinvested, whether real production is taking place, whether wealth is being created, and whether the macro-economy justifies the announced expectations and projections.

Causes for Worry

Of course, many worrisome economic signs are still with us. Here is a list of a few:

A. Unused and overbuilt capacities in several sectors of the economy

B. Rising unemployment

C. High levels or corporate and household debt

D. Declining productivity rates

E. Declining consumer confidence and consumption levels

F. Declining production and investment activity

G. A sclerotic Europe that does not want to change and lead

H. A faltering Japan that holds back Southeast Asian economies

I. Falling corporate earnings

J. A Federal Reserve that still does not grasp the consequences of its actions—that by cheapening the currency and overextending credit, it creates new economic threats

Causes for Optimism

The following list reflects my belief that although the worst may not be behind us yet, the end of this economic cycle is coming.[4] Unless we position ourselves now for bouncing back, we will miss the opportunity of the truly new era:

A. People have started understanding that wealth is not created overnight.

B. True production of goods and services (construction, inventory, capital, education) is again becoming the engine of growth.

C. Japan has reached its economic bottom.

D. Governments have abandoned the peculiar policy of accumulating surpluses that serve no purpose.

E. The infamous "Wall of Worry" on Wall Street seems to be defeated.

F. The Fed's model of valuing equities now suggests an under-valuation of equity securities.[5]

G. Up to now, there was no partner to dance along with the Fed in its aggressive effort to stimulate the economy. Now that partner has been found—it is called government spending and targeted tax incentives that are growth-oriented.

H. Up to this point, the debt market (bonds) did not respond to the Fed's easing of interest rates. I believe that yields in the bond market now will experience downward pressure (especially because real interest rates seem to be negative), which will stimulate higher long-term earnings prospects, higher spending, and higher levels of confidence.

I. International cooperation has won over partners that could bear economic fruit in a new spirit of alliance.

J. Corporate profits will start rebounding in the next six months. Unless we position ourselves now, the boat of investment opportunity might leave without us.

K. Monetary stimulus by the European Central Bank (ECB) will cut the cost of capital in Europe, uplift corporate bottom lines, energize investment, and (if it coincides with American stimulus) support a resurgence of trade. To that we should add higher exports by Asian economies, which in turn will uplift those economies, since they are export-led growth economies.

L. Slumping stock prices have forced some good companies (both in the United States and in Europe) to trade below book value. This will attract merger activity, which in turn will create higher levels of business activity.

Where Do We Go from Here?

In the book of Numbers, we find a magnificent story that could be called, "Here We Go Again." The Israelites had been wandering in the desert for over forty years simply because they were afraid of the "giants" their spies had seen in the Promised Land. Their fear of the enemy made them lose sight of their goal and their destiny. That fear turned into negativism and eventually into a bitter experience of death and destruction. Only two men among the thousands were ready to cross the Jordan River and stake their claim upon the Promised Land. In chapter 32, Moses again asks the descendants of that first group of settlers to go with him to capture the land, but their response seems to be similar to their fathers'.

When will we start realizing the potential of our economic Promised Land? When will we start replacing fear with courage?

The Three Cs of the New Cycle

Presented November 2001

The American economy has experienced two stages of living in a **cocoon**. The first isolation took place between 1995 and 1999, which is known as the new technology era. Loud voices of excessive optimism prevented wise voices from being heard. Professional economists expressed their concern about the bubble that was forming, especially in the technology-related equities market, but few investors heeded them. That cocoon created an exuberance that drove the stock market to historically high levels. Investors paid no respect to independent thinking, fundamental analysis, or understanding of what makes, sustains, and distributes wealth.

The second stage of America's cocoon is where we are right now. Individuals and corporations are trying to understand the new dynamics of the macro-economy, yet they are isolating themselves and removing themselves from an active involvement in understanding the costs and benefits of doing business in this environment.

Everyone is wondering how long and how deep the recession will be and how robust the recovery might be. Last month was the twelfth consecutive month of decline in industrial production. Indeed, we have lost approximately 6 percent of our industrial output in the last twelve months, which is greater than the loss of the last recession of 1990–1991. Retail sales have declined significantly. Even Federal Reserve Chairman Alan Greenspan cautions congressional policy makers about the uncertainty of our current economic environment. However, even in this bleak situation, we can clearly see that the overcapacity that has been built in the last four or five years is already going through a phase of **catharsis**. Only through catharsis and cleansing will we be able to renew our economy and understand the strengths, opportunities, and threats of the macro-economy. Unless the economy is cleansed of overcapacity and inefficiency, we cannot have a new start.

Economic variables such asn business confidence, purchasing power, incomes, employment, production, and profitability are in a declining mode and have demonstrated the fact that we are living in a cocoon. The declining profitability of U. S. corporations clearly indicated that the economy was moving into recession when it was first observed in the third quarter of 1999. This is because falling profitability causes corporate expectations, employment, and production to decline. I believe living in the cocoon of declining expectations and weakening commitments necessarily leads into catharsis, and that's good news.

Firms have already made substantial efforts to cut back their unwanted inventories and excess capacity. By doing so, they are cutting their costs and are better able to absorb the hits of the recession. The catharsis has led us to price reductions. In addition, the catharsis has led to a loosening of monetary and fiscal policy. Interest rates have been cut to the lowest levels since the early 1960s. The fiscal stimulus planned for 2002, which will include tax cuts, extra spending, and emergency relief, will amount to more than 1.5 percent of GDP, the biggest fiscal boost to the economy since 1975. The kind of catharsis that has been happening primarily in the last quarter has started being discounted by the markets. That is why we have seen the markets start a mild recovery in the last four or five weeks.

The catharsis is also reflected in the industries' capacity utilization, which has fallen to approximately 75 percent, the lowest level since the early 1980s. This is necessary; in fact, it might be necessary to drop to a level of 73 percent before real recovery starts.

Decreased factory utilization is part of the normal process of getting rid of unnecessary inventories, equipment, and other illiquid forms of capital.

The catharsis is also reflected in the corporate financing gap, the gap between external and internal financing of capital spending. This corporate financing gap is approximately 2.5 percent of GDP. But as profits fall, lenders become more reluctant to extend credit. Firms cut back their investment plans, yet eventually they will be forced to use their existing capital. As more internal funds are used, debt levels will be reduced. That marks the beginning of the new recovery. I would say that today's historically high corporate financing gap is a **catalyst** that will help the economy grow and move out of the recession in the year 2002. Unless the investors position themselves now, they will miss that boat of opportunity. The profit recession that I mentioned earlier—in which the S&P companies' profitability has declined by at least 50 percent—is also part of the catharsis. It makes corporate heads think twice about what investments they should make, how much to borrow, at what rate to borrow, and on what terms to borrow. This cleansing of the investment process also becomes a catalyst for new growth.

The bust that the economy has been experiencing in the last several months is not an effect of terrorism, but an effect of the economic and financial imbalances that were created in the mid- and late-1990s. Firms overinvested and overborrowed on the basis of inflated expectations, and that backfired. At the same time, households borrowed heavily, believing that their wealth had risen due to the inflation of their stock portfolios. These kind of excesses take time to unwind. However, people have started to understand how wealth is created. Businesses have started understanding how investments need to be made. Corporations in general have started to understand that exuberance and inflated expectations do not lead to real growth, but to an economic bust.

To some extent, I would dare to say that the terrorist attack on the United States became a catalyst for growth because both the fiscal and monetary policy became more relaxed and more balanced. Fiscal stimulus as well as monetary stimulus will likely spur spending, borrowing, and optimism.

The three Cs of the new cycle—**cocoon, catharsis,** and **catalyst**— are not strictly phenomena of the American economy, but are global phenomena. To a large extent, the economies of Southeast Asia also have been in a cocoon for the last three years. The sleepy Japanese economy is still in a cocoon because the Japanese still do not want catharsis in the banking sector to take place. From an optimistic prospective, though, it appears that the global economy is in a stage of synchronized catharsis. The bad elements have been largely taken away and the cocoon phase of this cycle is approaching an end.

We do see positive signs in Japan and in other Asian countries, such as South Korea, Taiwan, and China. As an observer of international markets, I would say that these are good markets for investment as we speak. They have been isolated enough, and now that catharsis is starting its time to move in. When the catharsis is over, the catalysts will regenerate the economy. So individuals, corporations, and mutual funds should invest in such markets during the phase of catharsis. That's the phase our American economy is going through right now. Japan, South Korea, and Hong Kong are also beginning the catharsis phase, and the rest of the Chinese economy has a potential of entering this phase in the next ten years.

I mentioned the corporate financing gap. Please allow me to mention another gap, the global output gap, the difference between the world's current output level and its potential output level. This gap has increased to its widest level since the early 1930s, which implies high excess capacity. This also implies high unemployment. Some would add that it might imply deflationary pressures in the economy, in which prices will fall, heading to lower production levels, lower profitability, and lower employment. However, I would say that this global output gap has reached its maximum. The catharsis is beginning through fiscal stimulus, higher volumes of trade, and looser monetary policy, which will act as counterforces to deflationary pressures.

What are the lessons for us as we see cycles of cocoon, catharsis, and catalyst in the economy? I would say the first lesson is: Stop thinking inside the cocoon. We need to think globally, invest globally, and diversify globally. We need to be observing the close economic connections between ourselves and the rest of the world. Getting rid of our cocoon mentality is necessary, especially if uncertainty prevails in the U. S. market for months or years to come due to the war on terrorism. Being isolationist in our thinking at such a time would be a great mistake.

The second lesson we can draw from this cycle is: Always think of counterbalancing strategies. These days we see the catalyst of a loose monetary policy; we have a fiscal stimulus package that could continue for several months. At the same time, raw material prices are rising and could possibly lead to higher inflation. What do we do? In case inflation hits, we need to hedge against that possible threat. How? Possibly by buying inflation-index bonds. This counterbalancing act protects against the risk of higher inflation. (Note also that these inflation-index bonds have been a pretty good investment in the last year or so.)

The third lesson: Adopt a countercultural mentality. A counter-cultural mentality says that when others move into a cocoon, we have already moved into the phase of catharsis. Others are moving into the catharsis, we have already moved into the catalyst. In our personal and corporate strategy, we need to routinely adjust and mix our portfolios in order to maximize our diversification benefits. We need to carefully select nontraditional asset classes that can help boost returns and create a portfolio whose sum is less risky than its parts.

Thinking in a countercultural, counterbalancing way, let's consider what is happening in China, as well as in India, Botswana, and Ecuador. If we had adopted this type of thinking in the last twelve months, we would have seen that international small-cap value funds have had a very low correlation with the movement of the S&P 500. Their expected returns are much higher than those of the S&P 500 over the next five to seven years. Furthermore, we would have observed that emerging markets' debt securities have had low correlation with the S&P 500. These observations suggest that it may be time to invest in these kinds of funds.

Even in the United States, the counterbalancing, countercultural mentality leads us to allocate parts of our portfolio to assets that have low correlation with the S&P 500. What kinds of assets are those? Treasury inflation-protected bonds and securities have a correlation of less than 5 percent with the S&P 500. Also, hedge funds have a very low correlation, usually less than 3 percent with the S&P 500.

In this category, I would also mention real estate investment trusts (REITs), which have a correlation of between 25 and 28 percent with the S&P 500. In the last year, REITs have definitely outperformed the S&P 500, and they are expected to continue to do so over the next couple of years. Real estate investment trusts are liquid because they trade like stock exchanges. Investment and commercial properties are required by law to pay out at least 90 percent of their earnings to investors as dividends, and currently they are yielding between 7 and 8 percent. Such an investment is a good example of counterbalancing, countercultural thinking because, if inflation indeed hits, rents usually go up with inflation. I would say the typical REIT dividend yield of 7 to 8 percent is very good in this market. I have a word of caution, however: real estate investment trusts should be selected carefully because they need to be based on properties whose fortunes are running contrary to the cycle of the economy. I wouldn't suggest, for example, a real estate investment trust in hotel or vacation properties right now.

Let me continue to address this combination of counterbalancing, countercultural thinking by saying that it would not be a bad idea to invest in mutual funds that have taken a real beating in the last year or so, but that have the potential of realizing tremendous gains over the next four or five years without any tax liabilities. More specifically, when mutual funds have tremendous gains and they distribute capital gains, the investors in the mutual funds pay taxes on those capital distributions. However, when mutual funds have experienced (as happened this year) significant losses, we can claim those losses on our portfolio only if we sell those shares. The fund managers themselves cannot claim a tax credit. However, they can balance those losses against future earnings and future profits. Look for funds that are pursuing this strategy. Such a red-ink fund gives you the potential of realizing both capital gains and tax savings. As the fund rises, the portfolio manager applies the accumulated losses to offset the gains. Therefore, the manager does not have to pay out any capital gains for several years and the investor saves taxes.

I close by sharing a thought I have about a potential catalyst for the market. This catalyst is hedging, using the short-term instability of the market for long-term profitability by employing LEAPs, which give an investor the right, but not the obligation, to be involved in the futures market by using derivatives. This becomes a counterbalancing catalyst for long-term stability. For example, say that Intel stock is trading at twenty dollars and you think the stock is going to thirty dollars within the next eighteen months. You can buy a LEAP call, which gives you the right to buy the stock at a pre-agreed price during the period of eighteen months. Perhaps the LEAP call option entitles you to buy the stock by February of 2003 at a price of twenty-two dollars a share. Instead of paying thirty dollars in 2002, you have purchased the right to buy it later at a much lower price. The call option definitely costs something, but it balances out the short-term risk of your portfolio and therefore increases your long-term potential.

On the other hand, suppose you are more pessimistic about the market. You then can buy a LEAP put, which gives you the right, but not the obligation, to sell shares at a specific price. So if you own Intel at twenty dollars and you are not sure where the market is going, you can hold onto the stock, but for a price (an insurance premium if you will), you can buy a put option for the long term. This gives you the right to sell the stock at a predetermined price— let's say eighteen dollars—and therefore you minimize your potential losses. I think that as more investors use such options as a counterbalancing long-term strategy, this could become a catalyst for the future.

The Swings and Moods of the Market: A Preliminary Outlook for 2002

Presented November 2001

This chapter has three primary sections. The first is about the future of the American financial markets. The second is about the swings and moods of those markets and the fluctuations that we have been observing recently. The third has to do with some particular investment strategies in the current economic climate.

Let me start by saying that the American economic climate before September 11, 2001 was already pessimistic. The debt and equity markets had dropped substantially because of over-built industrial capacity, low consumer confidence, cautious business leadership, low consumer confidence, the debt that hung over corporations and households, and the fact that the rate of return on existing investments was dismal.

We need to remember that this pessimistic climate was to some extent (if not to a large extent) the result of the change that had been observed in the mood of the Federal Reserve. The Fed started raising interest rates in 1999 and continued doing that into the year 2000. The Fed was pushing interest rates to higher and higher levels. This coincided with the over-built business capacity that had been created by American corporations as well as corporations around the globe.

The exuberance that existed from 1997 until early 2000 quickly turned into pessimism. It didn't just fade away; it turned around.

On January 3, 2001, the Fed started cutting interest rates, believing that our economic problems were monetary problems. Once again, the Fed clearly misunderstood the dynamics of the economy because it cut interest rates several times yet failed to move the markets.

Where Do We Stand Now?

The terrorist attacks of September 11, 2001 were expected to exacerbate this pessimistic investment climate. That is why we saw, in the first ten days after the markets reopened, that the Dow Jones Industrial Average dropped from about 9,500 to 8,500. However, since then, we have seen a climate of growing investor confidence. This can be attributed to several factors: winning the war in Afghanistan, lower interest rates, increased government spending, better consumer sentiment, better corporate earnings forecasts, more optimism about the economic future of Southeast Asia, and the appearance of the euro, which brings something new to the financial markets. It seems that we are moving the pendulum suddenly from pessimism to optimism.

I do have a concern about this, because such radical swings in the markets are unhealthy. Benjamin Graham taught us that investing is like dealing with a person called Mr. Market. At this time, Mr. Market seems to be a manic-depressive person whose mood vacillates between enthusiasm and fear. Sometimes, Mr. Market's price is wildly above any kind of fundamental value, and so he keeps buying and buying and buying, in an exuberant spirit that brings asset-price inflation—i.e., stock market inflation. On the other hand, Mr. Market's mood can suddenly change from enthusiasm to fear, and he starts selling at prices that are far below the intrinsic value of the corporation.

In the first case, when Mr. Market is extremely enthusiastic, it is time to sell. In the second case, when Mr. Market is fearful and pessimistic, it is time to buy. Of course, the trick is to find out the current temper of his mood.

Traditionally speaking, wartime makes Mr. Market more volatile than usual because of despair regarding the economic outlook. That is what happened after September 11. However, the pessimism has turned into euphoria as we approach Christmas and the markets seem to believe that recovery is knocking at the door. We can clearly see by any chart that the markets are sharply higher than their September 21 lows.

From a historical perspective, especially since the mid-1930s, a rally of this size and speed is unusual. We are only four or five months (officially) into a recession. So this is not a usual rally.

However, a rally like this signifies that the end of the recession indeed may be near. If we look at the last 65 years, rallies that preceded the end of a recession by 4–5 months led the markets to an appreciation of 12–15 percent. If the market will rally in this manner again, it definitely would signal that the recession is over.

Also looking back over the last 65 years, we find that the shares that gained the most value in post-recession rallies are the ones of companies with small capitalization. So small-cap stocks seem to be a good way that someone could invest for the next three or four months. We have observed in recent weeks that the price of bonds, irrespective of their maturities, have started falling.

I believe that, in the next eight months, it would be a good idea for an investor to park some money in bonds. Irrespective of fears that a strong recovery and strong economic growth may lead to higher inflation, I don't think we need to have such fears for at least another 6–8 months. We will see recovery and growth, but not strong growth.

On the other hand, someone may say that sudden swings of the markets create too much risk for any investor. That may be true. However, I believe we have overdone our optimism about a swift and sweet recovery.

Upswing Statistics

Definitely, there is good news regarding the American economy. The following data give us a portrait of these positive signals:

- The Purchasing Managers Index, which signifies the confidence level of corporations regarding the future, has stopped declining and started rising slowly.

- Despite the past instability of the Consumer Confidence Index, we now see it becoming stable and slowly rising.

- The yields on junk bonds have fallen in recent weeks. The gap between the yields on investment credit bonds and junk bonds has narrowed, which also signifies that the end of the recession is near.

- History teaches us that long expansions usually are followed by short recessions, especially if the interest payments of corporations and households are low, relative to their income and cash flow. That seems to be the case in this recession.

- Some types of manufacturing activity are picking up steam, particularly auto production.

- The level of inventories has declined.

- The Philadelphia Semiconductor Index is up more than 35 percent in the past 40 days, which is a positive indicator for the technology sector.

- Oil prices have remained low. Stable oil prices help us come out of a recession quicker, because they lower our energy and transportation costs, which account for as much as 15 percent of the overall cost of the economy.

- Other commodity prices hit the bottom on October 23, and they have returned to the level where they were before the terrorist attacks. The price of copper has risen by 12 percent in the last three weeks. I believe this is a clear indication that the end of the recession is near, because copper has always been a useful indicator regarding the economic future.

- At the beginning of November, futures contracts for the Federal Funds rate indicated a cut the next time that the Fed meets on December 11. However, the futures contracts now indicate that the probability of this cut is less than 30 percent. (A word of caution: It is possible that the markets are being driven by factors other than expectations about corporate profitability, consumer confidence, and the investment climate. At this stage, the bond market is a bit confused. However, the prices of both debt and equity securities have been bid up by the cash that had been parked for awhile in money-market funds.)

Some Investment Recommendations

Earlier, we talked about rebalancing some of our investment portfolios and we suggested keeping a reasonable percentage in debt instruments such as bonds. Perhaps as much as 20 percent of an individual investor's capital should be in the bond market.

At the same time, I see two significant things happening in Europe. The first is that the euro goes into official circulation on January 1, 2002. This will definitely increase the demand for euros and will reallocate global investment portfolios toward European funds. I would suggest that a portion of your investment portfolio should be in European funds and denominated in euro currency. I expect that the euro will be close to parity with the dollar in the coming year. If so, that would cause the euro to grow in value by about 11 percent, which is a good return on any investment portfolio. The second good thing about Europe is that, historically speaking, the price-earnings ratio of European stocks is around 16, which is much lower than the price-earnings ratio of Japanese stocks, which is close to 55. This is another reason why part of your portfolio should be invested in Europe.

Given the instability of the equity markets, as well as the everlasting change in mood of the markets, I suggest that it wouldn't be a bad idea to identify some companies that have the following two characteristics. Investments in such companies may protect us from a bear market.

First, we should look for companies with a high dividend yield (in other words, companies that pay high dividends while having low debt). I would say that a company has a *high dividend yield* if its yield is above 3 percent while its dividend growth rate is at least 10 percent. Companies such as Commerce Group, Chemical Financial, Lincoln Electric, Mercury General, and others have high dividends and high dividend growth rates while their debt-to-equity ratio is low.

Second, we should look for companies with a *low debt-to-equity ratio*. By this, I mean a ratio of 15 or less. Examples of such companies would include Lincoln Electric, Kimball International, and Commerce Group.

Bethlehem's Reversal of Values

But you, O Bethlehem Ephrathah, are only a small village in Judah. Yet a ruler of Israel will come from you, one whose origins are from the distant past (Mic. 5:2, New Living Translation).

We stand in awe when we read this prophecy—written in approximately 700 B.C.—that the Messiah would come from the small village of Bethlehem. God indeed chooses the unconventional to challenge the conventional. Jesus' appearance on earth threw everything off balance. The reality of "God with us" (Matt. 1:23) that started in the small town of Bethlehem unleashed a stunning reversal of values that went on to affect the entire world. The fact that the world honors and cares for the marginalized and the disenfranchised is a direct result of the birth of Christ.

Two millennia later the reverberations have not stopped. In a culture that glorifies success and grows deaf to suffering, Bethlehem's manger is a constant reminder that at the center of God's kingdom hangs a resurrected Christ whose story cuts against the grain of every heroic story. We are accustomed to celebrating strong heroes, not weak victims. However, Bethlehem's manger reminds us that Christ from the very beginning took the side of the weak. The Son of God was born in poverty and disgrace, spent His infancy as a refugee, lived in a minority race under a harsh regime, and died as a prisoner unjustly accused. Bethlehem made the cross of Jesus' sacrifice a reality, and through His sacrifice our hopes that we will live with God forever become alive. Bethlehem shatters the long-standing categories of weak victims and strong heroes, for here the victim emerges as the hero.

The Political Economy
of the Kingdom of God

At the dawn of the twenty-first century, the world's socioeconomic pathologies reflect the spirit of narcissism: Global unemployment has reached its highest level. Economic inequalities have exploded. Hunger has taken a fanatic face. Educational achievements have declined. Culture wars occupy the headlines. Social institutions promote selfishness. Poverty afflicts many more persons. Greed has been institutionalized. Fiscal and monetary policies have not only lost their cultural autonomy, but they have also become destabilizing forces in international markets. Natural resources are being depleted. Labor market policies promote the segmentation of society. Compassion is seldom seen in the marketplace. All of these socioeconomic pathologies are a prelude to the contemporary malaise of the spirit's bureaucratization.

The current ordering of social priorities produces irrational economic policies and uncertainties, while at the same time contributing to economic fragmentation among communities and nations. This chapter establishes links between the explosion of these pathologies and the failure of social institutions. It questions some of the founding premises of today's conventional economic thought, such as the principle that inequality generates economic prosperity. It calls for a renewal of the most significant social institutions, which would nourish the character of economic policies and build a framework for renewed economic synergism based upon the values of the community.

Socioeconomic renewal has to do with the inner resources of the culture. I reject the Chicago-based moral philosophy of rational choices, because it produces a totalitarian science in which everything is reduced to monetary figures. Such an economic ideology turns human beings into relentless market maximizers. It undermines not only our families, our neighborhoods, our schools, and our corporate culture, but also our economy. Instead, I wish to propose in a preliminary way how we might establish a Christian framework of economic analysis that is concerned with issues of social equality, shared values, global neighborhoods, shared power, spheres of life in which money is not significant, the practical denouncement of rugged individualism, social responsibility toward other persons and the environment, a transcendence of dignified paternalism, and a movement into a political economy of accountability.

The reconstruction of our social infrastructure must be accompanied by a restoration of the integrity of public institutions and by a rejection of the radical individualism that views life as an interaction of snatching and hoarding in which the self is the most significant social unit. Such a reconstruction will be based upon the virtues of a partial socioeconomic justice that ultimately leads to responsible impartiality.

At the center of any theory of political economy, one must deal with basic issues such as production, distribution, liberty, productivity, employment, growth, and opportunity. However, if we consider these questions apart from the sociocultural framework, we will develop a political economy which does not consider the dynamics of social institutions, ultimately resulting in an economic policy vacuum.[6]

Moreover, if we fail to incorporate ethical and moral valuations into our framework, we devise a hedonistic context of analysis in which production cannot be separated from robbery.[7] Unless moral standards guide economic policy, our answers to the ultimate economic questions will lack epistemological and ontological foundations. Furthermore, if the conceptual framework of economic policy lacks teleological perspective, it will fail to see the whole person's ultimate potential.

In this chapter, I will present the fundamentals of a political economy in which public economic policy is rooted in a Christian understanding of kingdom stewardship. I will integrate dynamics of social institutions with the cultural dimensions of these issues, for the purpose of exploring a paradigm at whose center lies the realization of God's kingdom. The paradigm will take into account the fundamental elements of human society, as well as the underlying principles and constructive features of a kingdom economy, all integrated into a building block of practical public policy.

The Surrounding Elements

From the beginning, I must underscore the fact that I recognize that there are several models of the kingdom of God.[8] Throughout the centuries, Christians have interpreted the kingdom differently. However, one common element that we can identify in all Christian models is the pursuit of justice. In the biblical framework, to seek justice is to live for the sake of the kingdom.[9]

We may define justice as contractual fairness in a framework of maximal utility, in which people are intent upon pursuing the common good in a way that the human spirit flourishes and rejoices by discovering God's purposes and plans. This definition combines several ethical traditions.

Another common element in various Christian models of the kingdom is the feature of community. God exists in community in the Trinity. He created us in His image to exist in community with one another. Therefore, the kingdom of God is a kingdom of community. We have been created in His image, but His image is a communal one. From this fact we may deduce several attributes of the Biblical politico-economic paradigm. Persons reach their full potential only in *koinonia* (fellowship) with others. At the core of any Christian economic policy lies the conviction that the kingdom of God is already at hand and involves a set of values that believers need to be live out now, in obedience to the gospel, by opposing the materialistic spirit of the age.

The third common element of Christian models of the kingdom is *shalom*, God's vision for creation. This term encompasses integrating the physical, the social, and the spiritual dimensions into the whole and redemptive work of Jesus Christ. Therefore, *shalom* in the political economy of the kingdom means harmonious, righteous stewardship that seeks to correct inequities, work toward economic justice, and bring hope to the hopeless. *Shalom* permeates the social and political realm by proposing an alternative social contract. The Sermon on the Mount, without being a detailed blueprint of the Christian economic paradigm, provides the moral framework of this social contract. Stanley Hauerwas and William Willimon write that the sermon is "the inauguration manifesto of how the world looks now that God in Christ has taken matters in hand. And essential to this is an invitation to all people to become citizens of a new Kingdom, a messianic community where the world God is creating takes a visible, practical form."[10]

The fourth common element of various Christian models of the kingdom is its prophetic and subversive nature. The new social reality of the kingdom is a countersystem of discipleship in which fidelity to Christ is accompanied by a radical commitment to the prophetic reality of restoration and reconciliation. Kingdom people not only lament with the disadvantaged and marginalized, but seek to restore God's ideals into our society.[11]

If an economy is a human reality, then economic questions are inevitably moral in nature. A society may tolerate (in the name of efficiency) hunger, poverty, hopelessness, insecurity, and injustice; but its moral conscience must reject these forms of modern economic violence.[12] In the naked public square of political and economic institutions, our Christian economic paradigm seeks to transform these harsh social realities.

Underlying Principles

Given the fact that God's rule includes the political, economic, and social domains, it is imperative that the principles of a Christian political economy be understood in the light of Scripture. I reject a theocratic notion of the kingdom, in which God's people rule in all spheres of life.[13] However, God's light and salt should permeate society, in order to preserve a well-regulated social order that supports a government that operates on moral grounds for the sake of the public welfare. This is the first principle of the Christian economic paradigm: *Our role is to permeate and influence society, not to govern it.* The church should be separate from the state, demonstrating Christ's redeeming role, transforming society's values by shining His light. The church's shining light is the servanthood attitude of all Jesus' disciples, who comprehend that creation is directed toward a final union with God, the intelligent Creator (Luke 22:26–30).

That servanthood attitude directs Christians to identify with the least and the poorest (Matt. 25:31–46). This is our second principle: *Because we are engaged in kingdom business, we identify with the poor, the oppressed, the marginalized, and the disadvantaged.* John Stott has said that while salvation is by faith and faith alone, judgment is by works.[14] The most obvious Christian work is solidarity with the poor. Christ himself is described in the Gospels as the One who identified with the least, the most humble, the most vulnerable, and the outcasts. He recognized (and we recognize) that the image of God is distorted if human beings are dehumanized by any form of economic violence.

God levels social inequalities, which are inspired and perpetuated by financial inequalities. (Note that the outcome of the Christian paradigm that I am describing is not economic equality, but social equality.) In modern society, money talks too much. It directs all actions and reactions. Money determines to a large extent the social worth of a person. Decisions related to social and public welfare are made by using monetary concepts in the absence of values, morals, and ethics. Economic inequality has been disfigured into social inequality. It is the latter that Christians should be against, because the Bible is against it.

Hence, the third principle of this Christian economic paradigm is: *We must work for social equality.* The concept has been rejected in America's political economy because we worship individualism. And, individualism is the main cause of our modern social malaises and pathologies. The root of nihilism is individualism.

Therefore, the fourth principle of the biblical political economy is: *We must reject radical individualism for the sake of sacrificial love and crucified interests.*

The Pursuit of Self-Interest: Is It Compatible with the Kingdom Paradigm?

Self-interest is the principal institution of modern market societies. We act as if we solely were in control of our destiny. Individualism proclaims, "I am self-sufficient. I am who I make myself to be. I am the master of my fate." Robert Bellah and his colleagues identified three types of individualism.[15]

First is ontological individualism. This concept was developed in the seventeenth century by John Locke, who said that the individual is prior to society. The ontological individualist believes that society is merely a collection of individuals.

The second type of individualism is the utilitarian. The first champion of this concept was Ben Franklin. The utilitarian individualist believes the goal of society is that everyone should look out for her or his own interest. Success is measured by social power, prestige, and material acquisitions.

Third, we have expressive individualism, which is the dominant form today. The individual is encouraged to cultivate the self and explore its vast social and cosmic potential. This is seen in individualistic hedonism and the search for self-expression and self-fulfillment. Persons are nothing more than self-centers who are looking for immediate gratification.

The destructive consequences of individualism are evident everywhere: lack of commitment, disharmony, broken families, institutionalization of vice, crime, exploitation, relativism that leads to nihilism, materialism, dichotomization of values, privatization of beliefs, and social chaos.

Unfortunately, the influence of individualism is found even in the church. A gospel of self-esteem and self-fulfillment is replacing the good news of God's kingdom. When our faith becomes a private matter, it is socially irrelevant.[16] With an individualistic faith, the values we live by tend to become personal and private. Absolute moral values disappear for the sake of meeting our own interests. The more we concentrate on our own wants and needs, the more we reap the effects of a warped character.

Moreover, individualism leads to loneliness. James W. Sire[17] writes that if we are forever attending to our own petty wishes, we will be left alone to attend to them all by ourselves. Even Christians suffer from loneliness brought on by selfishness. There is only one cure, and that is to start serving others sacrificially.

Radical individualism has led to radical subjectivity. In our society, everything is permissible. There are no absolutes, no ultimate values. Values are thought to be the constructs of human beings and human culture. Conventional wisdom holds that values cannot be found in any reality outside the human frame. We live in a world where the only source of value is the self. After Nietzsche, our society holds that the truth is just a "mobile army of metaphors." Nothing is thought to be really true except for the idea that there is no truth. Everything is a matter of social agreement. The end result is an ideology of utter relativism in which all values are equal. Thus, we see the link between individualism, relativism, and nihilism.

In the political economy of God's kingdom, radical individualism is rejected in favor of a radical commitment to the absolute truth of loving and serving others as ourselves. At this point, we can recognize the relation between the communitarian element of the kingdom and the principle of servanthood. Self-interest puts the self above the community, while loving servanthood sacrifices self-interest for the sake of others. This is the christocentric paradigm.[18]

Christian socioeconomic policies should take into account the principle of idealistic realism, that says that God's truth is ordered to merciful and partial justice. Biblical justice must be partial in order to restore impartiality.[19] Justice is tied to our identification with the poor, restoration of their rights and privileges, and the struggle for their advancement through sacrificial love by rejecting the bankrupt philosophy of individualism. God is the one "who executes justice for the orphan and the widow, and who loves the strangers, providing them food and clothing" (Deut 10:18 NRSV). Therefore, *we must be biased in favor of the powerless.* That serves as our fifth principle. At this point, we need to relate the principle of social equality to that of partial justice. The rights of the poor are the concern of righteous persons, while the wicked do not care about justice for the needy (Prov. 29:7). John Mason writes that "assisting poorer and weaker members of society constitutes a practical meaning of justice and righteousness is a theme running boldly throughout the Bible from the Mosaic laws…to the prophetic complaints…and reinforced in the New Testament."[20] For an excellent treatment of biblical verses dealing with the issue of poverty, see Ronald Sider's book *Cry Justice!* [21]

What are the rights of the poor? Definitely food, shelter, jobs, liberty, security, justice in the labor market and in the courts, education, participation in the cultural life of the community, rest, leisure, and removal of institutionalized injustices.[22] The possessive spirit of individualism that dominates today's market societies cares nothing about the rights of the poor. Yet those rights are not a utopian ideal, but a pragmatic necessity.

We need to remember that creation's goods are for all, not only for the privileged. When plutocrats control not only the money but also the culture and the democratic institutions, then economic inequality becomes social inequality as the basic needs of the poor are not met.

How then can we reconcile the spirit of the culture, moral socioeconomic priorities, and the ideal of justice? I believe it is exactly this three-dimensional question that bothered both Marx and Weber. Both of them dealt with the question of why capitalism emerged and developed in England. Specifically, they asked what differentiated England from other parts of Europe, allowing the growth of capitalism there? Marx analyzed the central features of labor power and surplus labor, the destruction of the peasantry, production for exchange rather than for consumption, as well as growing commerce and the propelling force of capital.[23] Yet all of these forces had existed for centuries. Why did capitalism emerge in the nineteenth century in England? In other writings,[24] Marx tried to rationalize the phenomenon by saying that the spirit of capitalism was already present long before the emergence of capitalism.

Max Weber, struggling with the same issues, suggested that the ethic of justifying the pursuit of profit had nourished the spirit of capitalism.[25] However, the institutionalization of injustices is related to the social relations of production and to the ultimate question of income distribution. Hence, we need to analyze the institutionalization of injustices and propose an alternative.

Economic Rights

At the outset, I submit that economic rights are a subcategory of human rights. Robert Nelson writes, "The notion that a person can be destitute and yet be civilly and politically free is a romantic myth."[26] Today's prevalent socioeconomic paradigm is predominately shaped by the misunderstood Weberian capitalistic ethos, neglecting economic rights. The result is that poor people have obtained a fistful of civil and political rights, but still have empty stomachs. Needy people are not free people when their condition prohibits them from exercising their potential as well as their role as equal members of a democratic state. Arthur Okun writes, "Starvation and dignity do not mix well."[27] According to Okun, every person, regardless of merit or ability to pay, should receive medical care and food in the face of need. I believe that the Christian paradigm could hardly disagree with such a principle.

However, skeptical voices say, "It makes no sense to call any particular distribution of goods 'just.'"[28] These skeptics contend that it is impossible to say how much income executives, lawyers, surgeons, or miners deserve. However, this is the complaint of a culture that rejects God's ideals and commands. The possessive individualistic spirit seeks the maximization of self-interests without considering the rights of the disadvantaged. The biblical ethos, as reflected in both the Old and the New Testament, cares for the needy and restores their rights.[29] The existence of human-created misery and poverty is an insult to God, the Creator and owner of all things.

Richard Gilbert writes that "there is a strong biblical tradition of challenging excess of wealth; at the same time a 'preferential option for the poor' can be discerned."[30] The early church's teachings on the issue of wealth, possessions, and poverty are clear. The church fathers insisted that redistributing resources for the sake of the poor was not an act of charity but rather the restoration of what was due to them. They taught that all economic resources belong to the Lord; their common cause and purpose asserts their common use.

St. Ambrose takes an interesting position by claiming that the wealthy are granted temporal goods (he even uses the example of Judas, who was given the moneybag) so by their misuse they will have no excuse after death. "They, then, who have devoted themselves to pleasures, luxury, robbery, gain, or honors are spectators rather than combatants. They believe the profit of labor, but not the fruit of virtue. They love their ease; by cunning and wickedness they heap up riches; but they will pay the penalty of their iniquity, though it be late. Their rest will be in hell." St. Jerome adds, "The apostle too tells us that covetousness is idolatry. Such is the climax of complete and apostolic virtue—to sell all that one has and to distribute to the poor, and thus freed from all earthly encumbrance to fly up to the heavenly realities with Christ....Let your praises come from the stomachs of the hungry and not from the rich banquets of the overfed."[32]

Following the early church's tradition, St. Thomas Aquinas was an advocate of a virtuous life that would guarantee a sufficiency of goods to all (what we call today social safety nets) as opposed to accumulation of goods in the hands of a few. Aquinas quotes

Ambrose: "It is the hungry man's bread that you withhold, the naked man's cloak that you store away, the money that you bury in the earth is the price of the poor man's ransom and freedom."33 Therefore, our sixth principle is: *We must establish distribution and wage policies that ensure that all basic needs are met.* This is not an equal distribution of all capital. However, it implies taxation on the basis of the ability to pay. Such taxation is based on the fact that resources and possessions are not ours but belong to a common cause. Unless Christians advocate fair taxation, zero-sum societies will be unavoidable. Economic equilibrium does not occur when supply equals demand, but rather when our claims (demands) are balanced by our supply of stewardship in the spirit of the collective responsibility that we carry toward our fellow human beings.

Constructive Features and Canons of Distribution

The canons of distribution in our economic paradigm should have the following attributes:

1. *The canon of social equality*. This is what Walzer calls "a complex theory of equality."34 Inequality in the money sphere will not create inequality in other spheres of life. Hence, the economic policy would be to limit the spheres of life where money talks, therefore limiting the significance of money. This canon would translate into treating all citizens equally. Otherwise, we perpetuate the maximization of self-interest and wealth accumulation at the expense of God's kingdom. It is clear throughout human history that the maximization of self-interest leads to segmented and polarized societies, while it leads all participants to view life as an interaction of snatching and hoarding. The latter has caused us to separate ethics from economic valuations, so production tends to be indistinguishable from robbery.35 Workers can no longer be treated as disposable elements (or, as our computer terminology calls them, peripherals) for the sake of maximizing stockholders' wealth. The restructuring and downsizing of corporations cannot be done at the expense of the workers' welfare because, if that is done, then we do have a zero-sum game. If somebody claims that

corporate downsizing is done because it will result in a greater good for a greater number of people, I would say that this purely utilitarian ethic is antibiblical and is atleast very questionable and doubtful, and at most a lie.[36]

At the same time, we need to underscore the logical trap that the religious right has fallen into. This group talks about the moral decline of American culture and the devaluation of society's ethical standards. It calls for a higher level of morality and family values. However, the religious right fails to address the root of the problem—that is, the victory of hedonism, the triumph of self-interest, the expansion of the role and significance of money, the radically individualistic and relativistic spirit that demands immediate gratification of the self, the culture of conspicuous consumption, the incarnation of greed, and the celebration of static impersonal equilibria.

The above short list of social pathologies has resulted in the loss of human dignity and has contributed to broken families. There is an internal contradiction between religious rights preaching of values and its failure to practice a value-filled life. The religious right supports and is supported by the cultural conventional economic paradigms, whose ultimate basis is social malaise and disaster.

2. *The canon of equitable production relations.* The second canon of distribution in this new economic paradigm emphasizes the nature of production relations. As was mentioned earlier, class divisions and conflicts have been created due to the nature of present-day production relations. Segmented and polarized societies are evident because the answer to the third basic economic question—for whom to produce, or distribution[37] is taken for granted even in Christian circles. The classic answer to the question of distribution is to let the market decide who will get the goods and services. Persons will be paid according to their productive contribution. Hence, money and goods will flow to everyone according to each person's ability. In such a system, everyone will try to get ahead by seeking the maximization of personal interests.

Goods go to those who are willing to pay the higher prices. The invisible hand—that marvelous concept of Adam Smith that combines self-interest with the price mechanism—is indeed at work.

However, we may pause and wonder: Does the biblical economic paradigm support production for our own sake? Clearly, all Christian economists would say that one of our first principles is stewardship,[38] because everything belongs to the Lord and we are caretakers of His creation. That principle is found throughout the Old Testament. Jesus in His teaching gives us the framework to answer the production/ distribution question. His central message is the coming of the kingdom through the atonement on the cross, which provides our redemption. If this is true (and there should be no doubt that it is), our lives should be centered around kingdom business, and our top priority should be to prepare the world to accept Christ's kingdom. Therefore, I assert that production is for the sake of the kingdom, and distribution should be made for the pleasure of the King. Only then will we "let your light shine before men, that they may see your good deeds and praise our Father in heaven" (Matt. 5:16). The Lord is clear that unless we "do away with the yoke of oppression, with the pointing finger and malicious talk" and unless we "spend yourselves in behalf of the hungry and satisfy the needs of the oppressed," our light will not rise in the darkness and our night will never become like noonday (Isa. 58:9–10).

In the biblical paradigm, what matters is for whom we produce the wealth (i.e., Christ) and how much is left for our interests when our giving is complete. This claim is based on the following scriptural passages:

a. *Matthew 25:14–30*. This is the well-known parable of the talents. One of the usual interpretations is that the parable talks about the spiritual charismata (gifts) of God's people and how we are supposed to use them for Christ's kingdom and glory. Christians interested in the economic application of the parable have argued that it establishes a biblical prototype for a valid and required rate of return, like the one found in asset pricing models.[39] It is well established that this parable, along with the one that precedes it (the parable of the ten virgins) and the teaching that follows (the story of the sheep and the goats), all refer to the return of the King, our Savior and Lord Jesus. They are all related to kingdom business. The bride (the church) is waiting for the groom, while the servant (the individual Christian) is taking care of his master's property, and the nations are awaiting judgment. The common denominator is that we are dealing with Jesus' business.

In the parable of the talents, the underlying truth is stewardship and production for the sake of the Master. The fruits of production do not belong to the servants, or producers, but are supposed to be returned to the Master. Hence, the question of "for whom to produce" has a kingdom-oriented, indisputable answer for a Christian. We produce for the King and we return the fruits of our productive capacity to the King. His expectations are high. Our use of the talents is a criterion for judging whether or not we can "take your inheritance, the kingdom prepared for you since the creation of the world" (Matt. 25:34). Did we use these talents to feed the hungry? to give a drink to the thirsty? To invite strangers in? To clothe the naked? To look after the sick? To visit the prisoners? To care for the least and the unloved?

b. *Luke 12:13–21*, the parable of the rich fool, says that "a man's life does not consist in the abundance of his possessions." The political economy of God's kingdom does not deny the entrepreneurial spirit, creative business engagements, or the responsibility of private property. However, it does deny the spirit of accumulation for self-interest, the spirit of consumerism, the spirit of materialism, the greedy pursuit of profit for the sake of profit, and the partaking in an easy life that shows lack of godly purpose and responsibility for God's business. The "take life easy" attitude of accumulatng for ourselves without considering the purpose of God in our lives or His calling to minister to the needs of the least is an evidence that we are not rich toward God. Denouncing self-interest and materialism is the essence of Jesus' commands that follow the parable of the rich fool (Luke 12:22–34).

The question of production and distribution is not just an economic question, but a moral one. It needs to be addressed on moral grounds in a framework of our openness to the transforming grace of God and our willingness to use our abilities, skills, talents, and property to prepare the world to accept His kingdom. Brockway observes that the modern economic person, in the majority of our contemporary economic paradigms, represents the incarnation of greed. Therefore, he says, our modern economic dogmas have become a dismal science.[40]

3. *The canon of permanent Jubilee.* The third canon of distribution is the canon of permanent Jubilee, based upon the notion that Jesus himself has become our Jubilee. The Jubilee concept as presented in the Old Testament (Lev. 25) was envisioned as an institutionalized mechanism of land redistribution for the sake of justice and public-policy fairness. However, as Sider has emphasized, "by the sacrifice on the Day of Atonement, the more prosperous Israelites were to liberate the poor by freeing Hebrew slaves as well as returning all land to the original owners."[41] The equalizing Jubilee mechanism was the structure that God ordained in order to show two things: first, that the absolute owner of labor and land (i.e., capital) is no one but God; and second, that the poor have rights equal to those of the wealthy. Jesus came and bought us on the cross by paying the ransom that God's justice required, which was nothing less than the blood of the Co-Creator. Hence, our atonement is permanent. The blood of Christ liberates us from our sins and entitles us to claim an inheritance in the kingdom. By Christ's sacrifice, God returned to us what He originally had designed and planned in the Garden of Eden.

Moreover, the year of Jubilee described in the Old Testament was related to the practice of living in the community that God had ordained. Since our community in the New Testament era is the church, and since we live in an era of permanent Jubilee, we should live in a spirit of Jubilee community where everyone has equal worth and value. In the biblical *koinonia* (community), the wealthy cannot live apart from the poor, but rather they engage in a life for the sake of the poor in order to use their talents for the relief of the least advantaged members.

While the Old Testament principle of Jubilee was a mechanism for economic equalization, I do not advocate income equalization. That is unattainable and wholly unrealistic. As Walzer has shown,[42] even an initial income equalization will immediately be translated into unequal distribution, given the different preferences of the economic participants and their agents. Instead, I advocate social equalization, in which the huge disparities of wealth are no longer translated into social inequalities. The notion of permanent economic Jubilee in our environment today means that we curtail the accumulation of wealth and money power, and we prevent these from becoming sources of inequality by limiting the spheres of life where money talks and votes. Isn't it interesting that the notion of social equality requires each person to have one vote, while in our modern market societies more dollars can generate more votes, and justice is more accessible to those who hold economic power?

Ludwig von Mises[43] argues (in what he calls the "law of the economic democracy of the market") that inequalities are justified and are a necessary part of the system because those who satisfy the wants of more persons will be rewarded more. However, this logic falls into the trap of circularity, because wealth goes to those who gratify the wants of wealth. Our social, economic, and political systems nowadays are designed to satisfy the needs of those with the most money.

Let's look at the example of the pharmaceutical industry. If von Mises is correct (that inequality is justified because those who receive the most capital satisfy the needs of more persons), why do we spend billions of dollars for maladies that afflict members of affluent societies such as the United States by doing in-depth research and by creating drugs and treatments in abundance for their citizens, while we neglect the diseases that destroy tens of millions of poor persons in the less-developed countries? Aren't poor people more numerous? Why do we ignore them? Von Mises argues that "those who satisfy the wants of a smaller number of people only collect fewer votes—dollars—than those who satisfy the wants of more people,"[44] but it is clear that the economic democracy of our modern market societies is deaf to the powerless because they have no money. Our system plainly values the affluent more than the poor.

This is the type of social inequality to which I am referring. It is produced and perpetuated by our current money mechanism and extremely unequal income distribution. I would have no problem with monetary inequality as long as the poor were treated equally, since we are all the same in the eyes of our Creator. However, when monetary inequality is used to create social inequality by governing all spheres of life, the system collapses under its own weight, as though controlled by a different kind of invisible hand that has a power of its own and does not allow people to decide what they need.

We need to build into the economic system not only permanent structures that curtail the power of wealth, but also institutions that restore the rights of the poor. We need ongoing social structures that insure the redistribution of power in favor of the least advantaged, in order to protect the partiality that leads to impartial justice.

4. *The canon of communitarian distribution.* The biblical communitarian model is found in the first four chapters of the book of Acts. The key biblical passages, which also support the notion that production should take place for the sake of the kingdom, are Acts 2:42–47 and 4:32–37. These passages deal with the fellowship of the first Christian believers. In the Jerusalem model, we observe the following:

a. It was not mandatory to give up one's property and possessions in order to become a member of the Christian fellowship. What mattered was the attitude that the believers had toward wealth and its use. The church fathers[45] sometimes equated possessions with sins. In the Clementine homilies, we read: "No one should possess anything, but since many have possessions, or in other words sins."[46] However, this was not the view of the apostolic Christian church.

b. The early believers' *koinonia* included redemptive economic relations. This had two important consequences. First, their state of mind related possessions to sins and the beleivers' fallen nature. Their oneness in spirit, heart, and mind was achieved when they no longer considered property and production as privately owned. Some of them may have kept their properties, but they were ready to liquidate them for the sake of the fellowship whenever there were needy persons.[47] Therefore, their bondage to mammon was minimized. They believed that property and riches enslave, while Christ liberates. They had long envisioned their return to the Eden prototype, where direct communication with God was an everyday reality. Since that communication was reinstitutionalized via the priesthood of all believers through Christ's sacrifice, the first Christians thought they had to separate themselves from any earthly power that could keep them apart from God's plans.

Second, the Jerusalem church understood that God's promise— "there should be no poor among you" (Deut. 15:4)—was fulfilled when the Holy Spirit came to stay with God's people permanently. "There were no needy persons among them" (Acts 4:34) due to the sharing that prevailed among Spirit-filled believers.

c. The Spirit of God convinced them that they could not have the love of God in their hearts and at the same time possess anything, because the possession would imply idolatry and lack of compassion. It would threaten their spiritual well-being, dissipating their God-given energy with the negativism of the proprietary attitude that prevails when self-interests surface.[48]

"They devoted themselves to the apostles' teaching and to the fellowship,…and the Lord added to their number" (Acts 2:42, 47) . This was the immediate result of the spirit of *koinonia*, their communitarian redistribution and economic solidarity based upon the community's needs.[49]

d. The prevalent word in the above passages is *koinonia*, which means fellowship in a spirit of sharing for the sake of the whole body.[50] In biblical *koinonia*, the collective well-being of the community supersedes the self-interests of individual members. Individuals cannot function without the community, and the community is healthy when the individual parts have healthy relationships with each other. Theissen argues that the conflicts within the Corinthian church were rooted in the contrast between rich and poor.[51] Hence, Paul's appeal for equality in 2 Corinthians 8:13–14 makes perfect sense, as he reminds them of the story of manna redistribution found in Exodus 16:16–18.

All believers are supposed to produce for the sake of the community and receive according to their own needs. *Koinonia* cannot exist outside the framework of social equality, which explains why Paul claims that the presence of hungry persons among the Corinthian Christians is a cause for God's judgment. Moreover, the absence of *koinonia* means that the Corinthians are partaking of a demonic cup rather than the Lord's Supper. "Do you despise the church of God and humiliate those who have nothing?" Paul asks (1 Cor. 11:22). The Corinthians' failure to recognize the body of Christ (v. 29) is rooted in economic exploitation. In contrast, true *koinonia* presupposes the absence of inequalities and would not perceive any class distinctions in the body of Christ.

The above features and canons of distribution help us to develop a framework of analysis in which public policy can mirror the community's endeavor to live by godly standards of love and social justice, being light, salt, and leaven in the world. The failure of Christians to engage in such public policy formation has had costly consequences. Carl F. H. Henry writes that such a failure "cast evangelicals in a pluralistic society in a role of concern only for their own special interests, and not for justice and equity as a public cause that embraces an evangelical agenda with that of all other citizens….Only public policy involvement that transcends a partisan agenda and envisions social justice as a universal due— reflecting God's universal demand for righteousness—can invalidate the complaint that evangelical orthodoxy is concerned for justice only when and as its own interests are violated."[52]

Therefore, we may ask, "What type of economic principles could Christians advocate on practical matters such as unemployment, the role of government, taxes, monetary policy, social safety nets, and international economic transactions?" Emphasizing that this is simply a preliminary treatment of the subject, I start with the role of government.

God ordained civil government as an institution to preserve justice, equity, and order. The elements explored in the beginning of this study—justice, *shalom*, and *koinonia*—should serve as guidelines in the exploration of other matters. We need to remember, however, that "the Christian counterculture disfavors all modes of social and economic organization in a fallen world."[53]

In order for government to preserve justice, equity, and order, it must engage in the production and distribution of goods and services, especially those that the market cannot produce, such as roads, the defense infrastructure, and services to preserve civilian order. Government must also be an active participant in formulating and enforcing any stabilization policies that are required to achieve the nation's ultimate objectives. Psalm 72 describes the ideal ruler as follows: "For he will deliver the needy who cry out, the afflicted who have no one to help. He will take pity on the weak and the needy and save the needy from death. He will rescue them from oppression and violence, for precious is their blood in his sight" (vv. 12–14). In this scripture, we again face the issue of how governmental leaders ("rulers") treat the least and the disadvantaged today. Violence can take many forms, one of which is economic. It can also be institutionalized (e.g., in slavery, wage inequity, etc.).

Therefore, Christians should advocate a government that cares for the least, demonstrating compassion for their afflictions.[54] Through taxation and conscientious spending (fiscal policy), the government should contribute to the objectives of justice, equity, and order by providing public goods and services, redistributing wealth to uplift the least, and stabilizing the economy in periods of serious cyclical uncertainties. The tax system should be guided by fairness (treating equals equally) and efficiency (providing incentives for work, savings, and productive investments that generate jobs). Only then will "the more important matters of the law—justice, mercy and faithfulness" (Matt. 23:23) be met. Indeed, the ultimate guiding principle of government policy (including taxation and spending) is economic justice. "Endow the king with your justice, O God, the royal son with righteousness. He will judge your people in righteousness, your afflicted ones with justice" (Psa. 72:1–2).

It is clear from such scriptures that God and His people can provide guidance to governmental authorities so that the goals of justice are accomplished via the fair provision of goods and services. If the tax system favors the wealthy and imposes a relatively greater burden on the poor in terms of their income and ability to pay, then such a system is unfair. It treats unequals equally. For example, a flat 10-percent tax rate would take relatively more money from the poor than from the wealthy, because the marginal utility and usefulness of $100 is much greater to a poor person who is making $15,000 a year than to an affluent one who is making $100,000 a year. In agreement with the writings of Pasquariello,[55] who has done an extensive evaluation of the American tax system as well as the U.S. Conference of Catholic Bishops,[56] I would argue that redistribution of income needs to take place in the form of progressive taxation.

Moreover, I advocate the principle of taxing all income and benefits, because in today's economy workers are treated differently from one another. For example, consider two employees, both of whom are making $25,000 a year. The first has excellent fringe benefits in the form of insurance and a retirement program, while the second has none. Moreover, let's assume that the first employee inherited some money and was able to buy a house, therefore gaining the advantage of tax deductions on mortgage interest. The second has no such benefit. This is clearly a case of treating equals unequally. The tax system in this case favors the person who is already better off.

According to the nonpartisan Congressional Budget Office, census and IRS data shows that the most affluent Americans collect more from the government than do the poorest persons. In the 1990s, American households with incomes over $100,000 per year received on the average $6,000 worth of federal cash and in-kind benefits, while households with incomes of less than $10,000 received about $5,000 worth.[57]

The political economy of the kingdom of God should not adopt the conventional wisdom on taxes, because that philosophy assumes that happiness is directly related to income. Such a direct correlation is simply unacceptable to Christians. We are not called to find happiness, fulfillment, and self-actualization in any material things, but only in Christ.

The issue of taxation and government spending is directly related to the previously discussed principle of partiality and to the principle of identifying and struggling for the rights of the least. Progressive taxation (assuming that it supports government spending that exercises sound stewardship and does not waste resources) curtails the power of money and the spheres of life where money buys influence. Hence, it is compatible with the principle of social equality. Progressive taxation goes hand in hand with the principle of production for the sake of the kingdom. Christians know that they do not own anything but the cross of Jesus. Therefore, if we produce for the sake of the kingdom and for the pleasure of the King, we should identify with Him who taught us that faithfulness is not measured by how much we give to Him, but by how little we keep for ourselves. That argument is clearly illustrated in the story of the poor widow (Luke 21:1–4).

Some may say that Christians are supposed to give sacrificially to the church and to the kingdom, but not to Caesar. I would say, "Amen!" It is the church's responsibility to take care of the afflicted. However, when the church abandons her mission, somebody has to do the job. God ordained civil government as an instrument of justice. Hence, the government should implement policies that favor the poor and the least advantaged.

The biblical economy displays preferential treatment of the poor. Revivals and spiritual awakenings have taken place when the church proclaimed the whole gospel, including Christians' responsibility for social justice. The proclamation of the good news should accompany calls for justice, equity, and the denouncement of injustice.[58] The lives of John Wesley, Charles Finney, and other great evangelists serve only as an introduction to the marvelous work that the Spirit of God can do when His people are ready to proclaim salvation by faith at the same time they denounce injustice.

John Wesley wrote that the gospel takes root among the poor more than among the rich. Specifically referring to the rich, he wrote, "Can the Gospel have a place where Satan's throne is?"[59] Later arguing for Christians to identify with the least, he wrote, "O how much better it is to go to the poor, than to the rich; and to the house of mourning, than to the house of feasting."[60]

Max Stackhouse, reflecting on the church's need to implement and seek a public policy that includes a preference for the poor, writes that the sins of the rich are much more threatening to the society's well-being than the sins of the poor.[61]

At this point, we should note the clear biblical mandate[62] that economically disadvantaged people have a responsibility to help themselves.[63] The institutions that seek to assist the least of our society (at both personal and structural levels) should first show them how they can help themselves. This is vital for the preservation of human dignity. In addition, while the market system is impersonal and mainly concerned with material values, it is not by nature evil. Persons who are engaged in unbiblical practices make the market system unjust.

The next underlying principle is the principle of full employment. I should note at this point that I reject the notion of NAIRU (non-accelerating inflation rate of unemployment, or simply "the natural rate of unemployment") on both biblical and economic grounds.[64] Without claiming that we can fine-tune the economy using a menu of choices among economic goals, as economists believed in the 1950s and 1960s, I would argue the following:

1.) There is no straightforward evidence that the markets can clear themselves of unemployment.

2.) Several market economies, such as those of Japan and Switzerland, have been enjoying full employment and stable prices for decades now. Therefore, something can be done to achieve full employment without any major effect on price level.

3.) There is clear evidence that the unemployed desire to have jobs at competitive wage rates. Therefore, the concept of voluntary unemployment is largely a myth.[65]

4.) Economic policy, both fiscal and monetary, can work effectively, as empirical evidence has shown.[66]

5.) The social consequences of unemployment make the economy inefficient. From a Pareto-optimal standpoint, the loss of jobs for the sake of higher corporate profitability clearly signals an   inefficient allocation of resources. The waste of human and societal resources, the health and psychological problems that unemployment generates, the loss of human dignity that occurs, the lawlessness that takes place, the breakup of families, and the loss of potential GDP all affirm that unemployment is one of the first social pathologies that nations should address.

6.) The trend of corporate downsizing and merging that has prevailed in the last decade contributes to the treatment of workers as liabilities rather than as assets. Such a view is anti-biblical because the Bible does not advocate concentration of   power in the hands of a few, as the Jubilee principle makes clear (Lev. 25:10,13, 23; Num. 36:6–9; Deut. 19:14; Eze. 46:16–18) Wilkinson writes that "the principle of avoiding the concentration of power is perhaps best expressed in a way meaningful to us today by the prophets Isaiah and Micah."[67] Furthermore, in a climate of downsizing and mergers, wages are no longer thought to reflect God-given productive capacity. Rather, they are viewed as variable expenses that need to be reduced. Thus, we suppose that we have a disposable workforce, and we leave people with no human dignity because we discount their productive capacities. Everything is reduced to monetary equivalents, which are manipulated to satisfy the desires of our greedy system.

7.) The Bible clearly has ordained authority to the leaders of civil government to distribute land (a means of production) so that every family will have land to work with and every individual will have access to the necessary means of life preservation (Num. 2, 26, 32; Josh. 13). In our modern society, the government also has the responsibility to create an environment of job generation, providing not only the incentives but also the structures and institutional support to preserve a fully employed workforce.

8.) The Golden Rule needs to be applied to unemployment policies. That rule should be safeguarded by the scriptural passages that prohibit exploitation of workers (Jer. 22:13–17; James 5:4) and mandate adequate wages for all workers (Gen. 31:7; Lev. 19:13; Deut. 25:4; Jer. 22:13; Mal. 3:5; Matt. 10:10: 1 Cor. 9:4; 1 Tim. 5:18).

The final economic principle that we mentioned has to do with international economic transactions and global policies. The fundamental features of the biblical economic paradigm with regard to international issues are the same as those followed in the domestic sphere. They are dominated by the element of justice. However, international economic justice takes a specific form that can be outlined by the following features:

1.) Persons living in less developed countries are to be supported with technological advancements, capital, training, and educational endowments in order to enable them to uplift themselves. Poor nations need to be helped by all means to secure self-sustained growth.

2.) Redistribution of income needs to take place, because the guiding principle is the production and reproduction of the greatest benefit for the least advantaged. To that end, monetary and fiscal policies suggested (and perhaps imposed) by international financial institutions should promote job creation. In addition, these policies should be designed so that the burden of economic stabilization does not become a yoke on the poor and the powerless. In the same line of argument, developed countries may forgo part of the loans made to developing countries, reduce the interest rates charged, or stop requiring poor countries to pay a large portion of their GDP to wealthy ones as part of the process loan repayment.

3.) We should not allow "big winners to feed their pets better than the losers can feed their children."[68] Global inequality and injustice have been well documented.[69] Over half of the world's population live, in the poorest countries, where the per capita GDP is less than $50. The combined GDP of these poor countries is less than 5 percent of the world's GDP. How could this be justified in a biblical environment where production is supposed to take place for the sake of the kingdom and used for the least advantaged? The poverty of poor countries is being perpetuated in the name of economic efficiency and growth. The needs of the poor are neglected in the name of structural adjustment. Furthermore, most individual choices and liberties are limited because the poor die young.

The institutionalization of global inequity has transformed us into one-dimensional persons who have no room for communal values in our self-centered societies. Moreover, Christians' defense of such ideologies contributes to dualistic and confused thinking, where the gospel has been reduced to a commodity and personal salvation is an egoistic affair that has no social relevance. True freedom cannot exist in the presence of social inequality, because freedom is destroyed by inequality. If such inequality exists, then the perpetuation of poverty will be the ultimate result, because the poor can never achieve a position of relative equality that would enable them to exercise the same freedom of choice enjoyed by the privileged groups.[70]

The following table shows this lack of freedom as a reflection of global income inequality.

Table 1
World Distribution of G.D.P. and Per Capita G.D.P. for 1999

Per Capita G.D.P.	Countries	G.D.P. (Millions)	Population (Millions)	Avg. Per Capita G.D.P.
Less Than $500	43	$933,000	2,857	$330
$500–$1,499	44	$500,000	612	$820
$1,500–$3,499	46	$2,466,000	985	$2,500
$3,500–$5,999	14	$114,000	22	$5,180
$6,000 or more	53	$17,658,000	896	$19,710
World Totals	200	$21,671,000	5,372	$4,030

Source: The World Bank, *World Bank Atlas* (Washington, D.C.: World Bank, 1999).

It is obvious from the above table that over half of the world's population lives in the poorest countries, where the per capita GDP is less than $500 per year and where their combined GDP is less than 5 percent of the world's total. This institutionalization of economic inequality reflects the modern manifestation of the "powers and authorities"(Col. 2:15)[71] that have revolted against God and His plan for equality and stewardship. Defending such inequality in the name of efficiency and growth manifests the demonic bent of our modern institutions. God's direction of justice and social equality is directly linked with a living church that upholds the standards of faith and opposes the institutionalized evils of inequality.

For countries such as China, India, Bangladesh, and Pakistan (which account for 40 percent of the world's population but less than 2 percent of the world's gross domestic product), the unequal distribution of income limits the freedom of individuals living there and undermines their potential. For example, in Bangladesh the GDP per capita is approximately $220 per year, a figure that represents less than 1 percent of the per-capita income of the United States. This inequality—whether due to differing skills, abilities, technological advancements, savings, innovations, capital accumulation, natural resources, or socioeconomic factors—results in nutritionally inadequate diets, primitive and crowded housing, an absence of medical services, and a general lack of educational facilities. Therefore, poverty is perpetuated. Choices (if they exist at all) are limited. Unreasonable burdens are imposed in the name of growth. The developed countries, instead of caring for things that matter such as educational level, birth rates, mortality rates, income distribution, technological advancement, the status of traditionally marginalized groups (such as women), impose on these nations austerity programs that usually lead nowhere.[72] The following table shows different measures of inequality for selected countries.

Table 2
Measures of Global Inequality in 1999

Country	Population Per Physician	% Adults w/ Secondary Education	% Adults w/ Higher Education	Debt Payment As % Of Exports
Ethiopia	78,780	15	1	8.9
Kenya	10,050	23	2	15.4
Nigeria	6,410	19	3	12.8
Bangladesh	6,390	17	4	8.0
India	2,520	43	8	16.0
Bolivia	1,790	42	7	16.4
Mexico	810	53	15	17.2
United States	450	99	63	5.0

Source: The World Bank, *World Development Report* (New York, NY: Oxford University Press, 1999).

From the above table, we observe the following:

1.) There are great disparities between the developed, the developing, and the poorest countries—not only in terms of their financial resources, but also in terms of their social conditions, employment growth, and human potential. This broad inequality feeds the decline of individual expectations and the culture of fatalism and despair.

2.) The gap between the rich and the poor produces a domino effect in the poorest countries, since low incomes of poor people affect their total quality of life.

3.) People in the wealthy civilized countries enjoy "the good life" and show a tragic degree of indifference for their fellow human beings who suffer in the poor countries. Worse yet, rather than helping them, wealthy countries blame the victims for creating their own predicament.

Table 3
Other Measures of Global Inequality in 1999

Country	Per Capita G.D.P.	Population Doubles (Years)	Labor Force % in Agriculture	Labor Force % in Industry	Life Expectancy (Years)	Mortality Rate Per 100,000 Births
Ethiopia	$120	25	80	8	50	2,000
Bangladesh	$180	29	56	10	51	600
Nigeria	$290	23	85	3	54	1,500
Kenya	$340	19	81	7	61	510
India	$360	34	63	11	58	500
Mexico	$2,490	30	23	20	73	92
Brazil	$2,680	37	29	16	69	150
United States	$22,560	89	2	28	80	9
Germany	$22,730	78	4	44	80	10

Source: The World Bank, *World Development Report* (New York, NY: Oxford University Press, 1999).

A few comments about the third table are in order:

1.) Impoverished nations not only are poor in physical capital (plants and equipment), but most important they are poor in social capital, as evidenced by the poor quality of public health[73] and education. These insufficiencies—and the indifference of developed countries to these problems—further destroy the poor countries' physical capital.[74]

2.) Human-capital deficiencies worsen the insufficiencies of the nations' infrastructure (highways, railways, sewage facilities, and so on). The ultimate result is an inability to make economic and social advancements.

3.) Illiteracy prevents national development, which leads to a spirit of dependency. Illiteracy maintains class distinctions and social inequalities. And again, the indifference of advanced countries to this problem perpetuates the trend.

4.) Terms of trade favor advanced countries, in the sense that exports from poor countries are subject to price pressures much more than exports from developed countries. This phenomenon makes poor countries subject to economic and political instability. Brazilian coffee, Nigerian oil, and Indian agricultural products are much more vulnerable to shifts in world prices than are American computers or Japanese cars. When prices of exported commodities decline, poor countries not only receive less money, but they also need to spend a larger portion of their income to obtain the items they need for their growth. The tragic fact is that the advanced countries, through their powerful position, push the prices of these commodity exports down.[75] Hence, they cause to some degree the misery that the poor countries suffer.[76] At the same time, international programs of debt restructuring increase the burden upon poor countries, which have to pay a higher percentage of their export income to service the interest being charged by the rich countries (see the last column in Table 2.) This practice is a complete violation of the biblical norms.

Conclusion

The irrationality of modern economic thought can be demonstrated by the fact that it operates under mechanical principles, rather than human principles.[77] The economy acts as the master, rather than as the servant, of the people. The people are shaped and taught to serve their economic system, rather than the system being shaped to serve the people. Moral questions such as prudence, benevolence, altruism, loyalty, commitment, integrity, and justice are thought to be irrelevant. The process of making economic decisions "does rule out a collective perspective, a perspective that considers what we should do."[78]

The political economy of the Christian paradigm does not allow this, because it cares for all people, especially for those who have been swept out of the mainstream of society. It values things that money cannot buy. It esteems moral values over social structures. It calls for people to focus on the ends rather than the means, and on the community rather than the egoistic goals of individuals. Social justice and social equality find their fullest expression within this framework because, in the biblical norm, concentration of power and wealth are signs of moral failure rather than signs of success.

Jim Wallis writes that we Americans did not become wealthy by sharing with the poor, but rather by loving the accumulation of wealth.[79] By contrast, a Christian paradigm of economics would restore the true meaning of wealth, abundance, and individual worth.

Notes

1. Editor's note: In December 2001, the American unemployment rate reached 5.8 percent, the highest since 1994.

2. The source of these graphs is the book, *Irrational Exuberance*, by Robert J. Schiller (Princeton, N.J.: Princeton University Press, 2000).

3. However, we do not know how much we can trust the official statistics about China.

4. Assuming that the "new war" is not prolonged and does not have any negative surprises.

5. According to this model, the earnings yield of stocks in the S&P 500 (that is, the expected earnings of companies in the S&P 500 index divided by the index's current level) is compared to the yield of a ten-year Treasury note. If the earnings yield exceeds the Treasury yield, then stocks are assumed to be undervalued, since it implies that investors are assigning less value to corporate profits that grow over time.

6. M. Tool, ed., *Evolutionary Economics: Foundations of Institutional Thought* (Armonk, N.Y. M.E. Sharpe, 1988); O. Hamouda and J. Smithin, eds., *Keynes and Public Policy After Fifty Years* (Aldershot, England: E. Elgar, 1988).

7. A. Sen, *On Ethics and Economics* (New York: Blackwell, 1987).

8. H. Snyder, *Models of the Kingdom* (New York: Abingdon, 1991).

9. E. Stanley Jones, *Christ's Alternative to Communism* (Downers Grove, Ill.: Abingdon: 1935); H. Snyder, *A Kingdom Manifesto* (InterVarsity Press, 1985).

10. S. Hauerwas and W. Willimon, *Resident Aliens: Life in the Christian Colony* (Nashville: Abingdon, 1989), 87.

11. C. Strain, ed., *Prophetic Visions and Economic Realities* (Grand Rapids: Eerdmans, 1989).

12. To that extent, the *National Conference of Catholic Bishops' Pastoral Letter on Catholic Social Teaching and the U.S. Economy* (Washington D.C.: United States Catholic Conference, 1985) reflects the subversive nature of the paradigm.

12. To that extent, the *National Conference of Catholic Bishops' Pastoral Letter on Catholic Social Teaching and the U.S. Economy* (Washington D.C.: United States Catholic Conference, 1985) reflects the subversive nature of the paradigm.

13. A primary reason I reject theocratic models of the kingdom is the hunger for power that accompanies them. Under most theocratic models, believers seek to obtain social and political power, then use it to force society to be righteous. However, Christ gave up such power.

14. J. Stott, *The Contemporary Christian* (Downers Grover, Ill.: InterVarsity Press, 1992).

15. R. Bellah, R. Masden, W. Sullivan, A. Swidler, and S. Tipton, *Habits of the Heart* (Berkeley: University of California, 1985).

16. O. Guiness and J. Steel, eds., *No God but God* (Chicago Press: Moody, 1992).

17. J. Sire, *Chris Chrisman Goes to College* (Downers Grove: Ill.: InterVarsity Press: 1993).

18. It could be argued that this principle is at the core of what Ronald J. Sider calls "incarnational Kingdom Christianity." See R. Sider, *One-Sided Christianity* (Grand Rapids: Zondervan,: 1993).

19. S. C. Mott, "The Partiality of Biblical Justice," in H. Schlossberg, V. Samuel, and R. Sider, eds., *Christianity and Economics in the Post–Cold War Era* (Grand Rapids: Eerdmans, 1994). See also S. C. Mott, *Biblical Ethics and Social Change* (New York: Oxford University, 1982).

20. J. Mason, "A Public Welfare Policy," in R. Chewning, ed., *Biblical Principles and Public Policy* (Colorado Springs: Navpress, 1991).

21. R. Sider, *Cry Justice!* (Downers Grove: InterVarsity Press, 1980).

22. Institutionalized injustices have been called the structural sins from which Christians need to repent. See R. Sider, *Rich Christians in an Age of Hunger* (Downers Grove, Ill.: Intervarsity Press, 1984).

23. K. Marx, *Capital: A Critique of Political Economy*, ed. F Engels (New York: International Publishers, 1967).

24. K. Marx, *Grundisse der Kritik der politischen, Ökonomie* (Texts on method [of] Karl Marx), trans and ed. T. Carver (Oxford: Blackwell, 1975).

25. M. Weber, *The Protestant Ethic and the Spirit of Capitalism* (New York: Scribner, 1976); M. Weber, *General Economic History*, ed. F. Knight, (New York: Collier, 1961).

26. A. Swidler, ed., *Human Rights in Religious Tradition* (New York: Pilgrim, 1982).

27. A. Okun, *Equality and Efficiency: The Big Tradeoff* (Brookings Institution, 1975), 17.

28. W. Kauffman, *Without Guilt and Justice* (New York: Peter Wyden, 1973), 67.

29. This point is clarified by Scripture passages such as Isaiah 58; 59; 61:1–2; Amos 4–8; Micah; Matthew 5, 6, 19, and 25; and Acts 4.

30. R. Gilbert, *How Much Do We Deserve?* (New York: University Press of America, 1991), 34.

31. St. Ambrose, *Nicene and Post-Nicene Fathers*, vol. 10: T*he Principal Works of St. Ambrose* (Peabody, Mass.: Hendrickson, 1994), II.

32. St. Jerome, *Nicene and Post-Nicene Fathers*, vol. 6: *Letters and Selected Works* (Peabody, Mass.: Hendrickson, 1994), 268.

33. Quoted by L. Schumacher, *The Philosophy of Equitable Distribution: A Study in Economic Philosophy* (Washington, D. C.: Catholic University Press, 1949), 62.

34. M. Walzer, *Spheres of Justice: A Defense of Pluralism and Equality* (New York: Basic Books, 1983).

35. A. Sen, *On Ethics and Economics.*

36. S. Danzinger and P. Gottschalk, eds., *Uneven Tides: Rising Inequality in America* (New York: Russell Sage Foundation, 1994); M. Kaus, *The End of Equality* (New York: Basic Books, 1992); F. Levy and R. Murnane, "U.S. Earning Levels and Earnings Inequality," *Journal of Economic Literature* (September 1992); L. Mishet and J. Bernstein, *The State of Working America* (Washington, D. C.: Economic Policy Institute, 1994); B. Bluestone, *Lean and Mean* (Basic Books: 1993); E. Wolff, T*op Heavy* (Brookings Institution: 1994); A. Glyn and D. Miliband, *Paying for Inequality* (Rivers Oram Press: 1994); "The Wage Squeeze," *Business Week*, July 17, 1995; "Inequality," *Business Week*, August 15, 1994.

37. The first two questions are what to produce and how to produce. While both are part of the political economy, I believe that

the question of distribution is the primary one related to the subject of the kingdom.

38. J. Tiemstra, "Christianity and Economics: A Review of the Recent Literature," *Christian Scholar's Review 22* (1994):3.

39. See among others W. Wood, "The Political Economy of Regulation," in R. Chewning, ed., *Biblical Principles and Public Policy* (Colorado Springs, Ill.: Navpress Press, 1991).

40. G. Brockway, *The End of Economic Man* (N. Y.: W. W. Norton, 1993).

41. R. Sider, *Rich Christians in an Age of Hunger* (Downers Grove, Ill.: InterVarsity-Press, 1984), 81.

42. M. Walzer, *Spheres of Justice*.

43. L. von Mises, *Human Action: A Treatise on Economics* (New Haven: Yale University Press, 1956).

44. Ibid., 10.

45. M. Henger, *Property and Riches in the Early Church* (Minneapolis: Fortress, 1980).

46. St. Clement, *Ante-Nicene Fathers*, vol. 8: *The Clementine Homilies* (Peabody, Mass.: Hendrickson, 1994), 311.

47. J. Gonzalez, *Faith and Wealth* (New York: Harper and Row, 1990).

48. Some claim that the economic *koinonia* practiced by the first church was nonsense. Among them are G. North, *The Sinai Strategy* (Tyler, Tex.: Institute of Christian Economics, 1986), and D. Chilton, *Productive Christians in an Age of Guilt Manipulators* (Tyler, Tex.: Institute of Christian Economics, 1981). Their main argument is that the Jerusalem model failed and the believers all became poor as a result of the inefficiencies produced by their communitarian way of life. However, I wonder where evidence of that is found in the Scriptures. Acts 11:27–30 tells us (and historians Josephus, Tacitus, and Suetonius confirm) that because of massive famines, poverty spread throughout Palestine and ultimately prevailed. The poverty had nothing to do with the communitarian spirit of the early church.

49. L. T. Johnson criticizes the Jerusalem model in his book *The Literary Function of Possessions in Luke-Acts* (Missoula, Mont.: Scholars Press, 1977), saying that the description in Acts is merely

an attempt to show that the early church was an ideal Hellenistic-Pythagorean community. I would briefly note the following:

a. The Hellenistic-Pythagorean model was formed to serve the purposes of the elite, while the biblical model was established for the sake of the poor.
b. In the Hellenistic model, membership was restricted to philosophers. The Christian church was open for everyone to come and celebrate God's kingdom.
c. It would have been foolish for the writer of Acts to record in A.D. 80 that the Jerusalem church had been organized on a communal basis if that were not so, because there would have been many live witnesses to dispute the claim.
d. If Luke wanted to idealize the Jerusalem community, why did he record the complaints of the Hellenists and the case of Ananias?
e. Gonzalez (op. cit.) notes evidence that the church continued to practice communal sharing long after the book of Acts had been completed.

50. C. Brown, ed., *The New International Dictionary of New Testament Theology*, 4 vols. (Grand Rapids: Zondervan, 1986).

51. G. Theissen, *The Social Setting of Pauline Christianity: Essays on Corinth* (Minneapolis: Fortress, 1982).

52. C. Henry, "Linking the Bible to Public Policy," in R. Chewning, ed., *Biblical Principles and Public Policy* (Colorado Springs: NavPress, 1991), 128.

53. J. Anderson, "Federal, State, and Local Taxation Policy," in R. Chewning, ed., *Biblical Principles and Public Policy* (Colorado Springs: Nav Press, 1991) 128.

54. This would comply with the biblical summons to justice, compassion, and sharing with the poor. See Lev. 19:33–34; 25:35-38; Deut. 5:14–15; 10:17–19; 15:7–11; 23:19–20; 24:17–22; Ps. 33:5, 41:1–2; 103:6; 146:5–9; Prov. 19:17; 25:21; Isa. 9:6–7; 32:1–8; 58; Jer. 22:1–5; Amos 4:1–3; Luke 4:16–19; Acts 20:35; Rom. 12:13; Gal. 6:10; 1 Tim. 6:18; James 2:1–10.

55. R. Pasquariello, *Tax Justice* (Lanham, Md.: University Press of America, 1985).

56. *Pastoral Letter National Conference of Cathoic Bishops.*

57. The revelations of Howe and Longman are astonishing. N. Howe and P. Longman, "The Next New Deal," *The Atlantic,* April 1992.

58. T. Smith, *Revivalism and Social Reform* (Baltimore: Johns Hopkins University, 1980); H. Snyder, *The Radical Wesley* (Downers Grove: InterVarsity Press, 1980); C. Finney, *Lectures on Revival of Religion,* ed., McLaughlin, (1960); R. Heitzenrater, *Wesley and the People Called Methodists* (Nashville: Abingdon, 1995); J. McManners, ed., *The Oxford Illustrated History of Christianity* (New York: Oxford University Press, 1990).

59. J. Wesley, *Wesley's Works,* vol. 3: *Journal* (Grand Rapids: Baker, 1991), 274.

60. Ibid., 224.

61. M. Stackhouse, "Protestantism and Poverty," R. Neuhaus, ed., *The Preferential Option for the Poor* (Grand Rapids: Eerdmans, 1988).

62. The biblical theme of gleaning in Leviticus 19:9–10 emphasizes that both the poor and well-to-do are responsible for searching for opportunities to feed the poor.

63. The latter is well documented in R. Chewning, ed., *Biblical Principles and Public Policy* (Colorado Springs: Nav Press, 1991).

64. Robert Eisner has done an excellent job of showing from both a theoretical and empirical standpoint that the N.A.I.R.U. is a myth. R. Eisner, "Our NAIRU Limit: The Governing Myth of Economic Policy," *The American Prospect,* Spring 1995. Also see E. Phelps, *Structural Slumps* (Cambridge: Harvard University Press, 1994).

65. D. Gordon, S. Bowles, and T. Weisskopf, *After the Waste Land* (Armonk, N.Y.: M.E. Sharpe, 1991).

66. A. Blinder, *Economic Policy and Economic Science: The Case of Macroeconomics* (Economic Council of Canada, 1988); A. Blinder, *Macroeconomics under Debate* (University of Michigan Press: 1989).

67. B. Wilkinson, "Biblical Principles and Unemployment," in R. Chewning, ed., *Biblical Principles and Public Policy* (Colorado Springs: NavPress, 1991).

68. A. Okun, *Equality and Efficiency* (Washington, D.C.: Brookings Institution, 1975), 1.

69. Just a look at the *World Bank Atlas*, published by Oxford University Press for the World Bank can verify the existence of global inequality and injustice.

70. A. Kirk, *The Good News of the Kingdom Coming* (Downers Grove, Ill.: InterVarsity Press, 1983); S.C. Mott, op. cit.; Kaus, End of Equality.

71. H. Berkhof, *Christ and the Powers* (Scottdale, Pa.: Herald Press, 1962); W. Wink, *Naming the Powers* (Minneapolis: Fortress, 1984); W. Wink, *Unmasking the Powers* (Minneapolis: Fortress, 1986).

72. P. Valley, *Bad Samaritans: First World Ethics and Third World Debt* (Maryknoll, N.Y.: Orbis, 1990); D. Grigg, *The World Food Problem* (New York: Blackwell, 1985); L. Osberg, ed., *Economic Inequality and Poverty*(Armonk, N.Y.: M.E. Sharpe, 1991); E. Eshag, *Fiscal and Monetary Policies and Problems in Developing Countries* (New York: Cambridge University Press, 1983).

73. See J. Hardoy, S. Caimcross, and D. Satterthwaite, *The Poor Die Young* (London: Earthscan Publications, 1990).

74. R. Levine and D. Rennett, "A Sensitivity Analysis of Cross-Country Growth Regressions," *American Economic Review* (1992) 82:4; P. Romer, *Human Capital and Growth: Working Paper No. 3173* (Cambridge, Mass.: National Bureau of Economic Research, 1989); P. Romer, *Capital, Labor, and Productivity* (Washington, D.C.: Brookings Institution, 1990).

75. In the 1980s, not only did wealthy countries push down the prices of goods imported from poor countries, but they also pushed interest rates up, forcing the same poor countries to pay higher interest on their loans and eventually weakening their economic structures. This might be considered a modern form of institutionalized evil.

76. *North-South: A Programme for Survival* (Independent Commisssion on International Development Issues, London: Pan Books, 1980); A. Sen, "Starvation and Exchange Entitlement," *Cambridge Journal of Economics 1* (1977) 1; A. Sen, "The Living

Standard," *Oxford Economic Papers,* No. 6; D. Hay, *North and South: The Economic Debate in the Year 2000* (InterVarsity: 1983).

77. P. Mirowski, *Against Mechanism* (Totowa, N.J.: Rowman and Littlefield, 1988); B. Griffiths, *The Creation of Wealth* (Downers Grove, Ill.: InterVarsity Press, 1984); R. Hamrin, "Ethical Economics," *Futures,* December 1989.

78. Hausman and McPherson, "Taking Ethics Seriously," *Journal of Economic Literature* 31 (1993): 2, 718.

79. J. Wallis, *The Call to Conversion* (New York: Harper and Row, 1992).

DATE DUE

Demco, Inc. 38-293